Early Christians of the
21st Century

Early Christians of the
21st Century

CHAD WALSH

GREENWOOD PRESS, PUBLISHERS
WESTPORT, CONNECTICUT

The Library of Congress has catalogued this publication as follows:

Library of Congress Cataloging in Publication Data

Walsh, Chad, 1914-
    Early Christians of the 21st century.

    1. Civilization, Christian.   I.   Title.
[BR115.C5W26 1972]   261   78-138136
ISBN 0-8371-5709-9

BR
115
.C5
W26
1972

ACKNOWLEDGMENT
The author wishes to thank the several publishers
who have kindly granted permission to reprint
extracts from their copyrighted works.

Originally published in 1950
by Harper & Brothers, Publishers, New York

Reprinted with the permission
of Harper & Row, Publishers

First Greenwood Reprinting 1972

Library of Congress Catalogue Card Number 78-138136

ISBN 0-8371-5709-9

Printed in the United States of America

For

BERNARD IDDINGS BELL

Damaris joins with me in this dedication

Contents

Foreword

This is a book about two things: the deathbed misery of one civilization, and the civilization that may be waiting to take its place.

Part One is an attempt to demonstrate that "modern civilization," which dates roughly from the Renaissance, is now on its last legs. This glum conviction is less startling than it would have been a few decades ago, when the doctrine of inevitable progress still had many adherents in both low and high places. Today the funeral bell is being rung by a whole army of philosophers and social scientists. I join their ranks not out of the desire to be in step or from a perverse love of the pessimistic, but simply because the facts seem to support their somber diagnosis. In my treatment I have not attempted a systematic listing of everything wrong with modern civilization (which would be too tedious) nor an enumeration of the things right with it. Instead, I have dwelt at some length on several of the outstanding symptoms of general old age and decay.

The second matter—the birth of a new civilization—involves numerous unknowns. Even if we assume that humanity will not eliminate its problems by eliminating the human race, we have no guarantee that a new civilization will rise from the broken juke boxes of the old. Perhaps we are headed toward barbarism, and the barbarism will be permanent. I shall run the risk of over-optimism and bluntly assume that history *will* repeat itself, that the death of one civilization will be followed by the birth of another. But this merely leads us to the main field of battle. Every man rushes forward displaying his blueprints for utopia. The technocrat with his vision of infinite leisure in which nothing interesting need ever happen; the wild-eyed apostle of the classless society; the wild-eyed archaist dreaming of knights, ladies, and dutiful serfs—all collide together in a bloody mêlée.

We might count noses, I suppose, and award the future to the most numerous band. However, history has a way of disregarding Gallup polls. This is what I hope and believe will happen this time. One of the least strident ideologies competing for the future is Christianity. Most of the advanced thinkers point out (justly enough) that the impact of Christianity has been on the decline for the past several centuries, and from this (with much less logic) they frequently draw the conclusion that Christianity will shortly fade away completely. An opposite conclusion can be drawn. Perhaps the present sad state of Western civilization arises largely from the watering-down and outright rejection of Christianity. In that case, a return to Christianity may be the price a reluctant world will have to pay if it wants any civilization at all.

However, I hasten to assure the agnostic reader that he is in no danger of being converted by this book. In an earlier work, *Stop Looking and Listen,* I explained why I believe Christianity to be true; I shall not go over the same ground here. My purpose is merely to show why I consider it highly probable that Christianity, whether one likes it or not, will emerge from the underworld of ideas within a

few generations—emerge with new vigor after its long
hibernation, so that the Christians of the twenty-first century will manifest the dedication and buoyancy possessed
in such a marked degree by the early Christians of the first
century A.D. I shall explain why I think this likely, and then
(in Part Two) I shall try, in somewhat more systematic
fashion, to imagine the impact that a rejuvenated Christianity may have upon the new civilization. In a word, what
would a post-modern Christian civilization be like? What in
it would seem strange to us? What features of modern
secular civilization would be retained, baptized, and re-
generated?

In reality I do not fear the wrath of the agnostics so
greatly as the outraged protests of many Christians. Agnostics, I find, often have a very lucid grasp of the main
doctrines of Christianity, and will readily admit that *if*
Christianity were true, it would logically have drastic
things to say about the market place, the studio, the classroom, and the marriage bed.

On the other hand, millions of Christians live in a sentimental haze of vague piety, with soft organ music trembling
in the lovely light from stained-glass windows. Their
religion is a thing of pleasant emotional quivers, divorced
from the will, divorced from the intellect, and demanding
little except lip service to a few harmless platitudes. I suspect that Satan has called off the attempt to convert people
to agnosticism. If a man travels far enough away from
Christianity he is always in danger of seeing it in perspec-
tive and deciding that it is true. It is much safer, from
Satan's point of view, to vaccinate a man with a mild case
of Christianity, so as to protect him from the real thing.

The word "Christianity" is so loosely used that I should
briefly explain what I mean by it. I have in mind the main

tradition of Christianity, centered in one supreme historical event: the Incarnation. Logically associated with the
Incarnation are such basic doctrines as Original Sin, the
Atonement, Grace, and Immortality. Taking the world as a
whole, this central Christian tradition is the faith of the
vast majority of believers.

I readily and gladly recognize that many Christians who
do not accept this central tradition would derive from their
concepts of Christianity social and cultural implications
similar to those that I find in classical Christianity. Indeed,
I would go further and say that a devout Jew, a devout
Mohammedan, or a devout Buddhist would very likely see
in his religion certain social ideas like those to be derived
from Christianity. There is an underlying ethos to most of
the great religions, which sets them apart from the shallow-
ness of secularism, and gives their followers many ideals in
common.

Throughout this book I speak only of the implications
of classical Christianity, but the reader should bear in
mind what I have just said. I have used classical Christianity
as the jumping-off point because I am most familiar with it,
and trust that it will be the prevailing form of Christianity
in the future. I have no desire, however, to suggest an
artificial contrast between the social insights of different
religious viewpoints.

I suppose I should say something about the atomic age.
A moment ago I assumed—all too glibly—that mankind
will not commit suicide. Race suicide has now become so
probable an event that the prudent man ventures no
prophecies. It is more than a possibility that a world-wide
atomic war between equally matched powers would destroy every last creature on the face of the earth. Or, if
that did not happen, the only human survivors might be a

handful of primitive tribesmen in unstrategic parts of the world.

But there is yet another possibility. An atomic war between two great powers, i.e., America and the Soviet Union, might end suddenly with total victory for the side better prepared or quicker on the draw. The winning side would then presumably dominate the world and remake it to taste. But that in itself would not change anything too drastically. Despite the invective they hurl at each other, America and Russia are first cousins under the skin. Both are secular nations with interesting vestiges of Christianity embedded in their civilizations; both worship the same gods of Power and Plenty. The winning nation would face singlehanded the ultimate decisions now confronting both.

Pessimistic speculation about the atomic age can be carried too far. There is at least a possibility that we will never have an atomic war. Every nation may be too fearful to start one. For the same reason, poison gas was not used during World War II. Most pleasant possibility of all, the world may stagger along without any major wars, so that a new civilization can arise without the total destruction of the present order.

No one really knows, and it seems futile to spend too many hours gazing at tea leaves. Since it is pointless to write this book if no one will be here to read it five years from now, or if the only survivors speak Congoese or Tibetan, I am obliged to assume that the world will not be too completely smashed up, and that the new civilization can be built, at least in part, on the technological and scientific foundations that we now have.

I am acutely aware of how presumptuous it is for one person to say *what* the Christian civilization of the future will be like. I have written this book only because the besetting sin of religious people is to talk forever of "principles" but never to get down to brass tacks. It is fine to say that a good society should be based on "love" and "justice," but the statement is not of much help to the politician or businessman confronted by complicated and urgent situations. I feel that it is better to hazard some guesses about the new civilization (though some of them are certain to be wrong) than to rest comfortably among the familiar platitudes. If this book provokes anyone into thinking his own way through the social and cultural implications of Christianity, it will have served its purpose. If it arouses disagreement, better still. The blueprints of the future cannot be drafted by one man or a handful of men. In so far as they are drafted by men at all, the more draftsmen there are at work, the greater chance that the design will be both Christian and workable.

I regret that I cannot make individual acknowledgment to all the people who have helped me in thinking out this book. I owe much to chance conversations with my colleagues, students, and other friends, but my memory fails me when I try to remember names and details.

In a few instances, however, I can be more specific. I am grateful to the Beloit Chapter of Phi Beta Kappa for asking me to deliver the address at the initiation banquet in the fall of 1946. My talk, the gist of which appears here as "The Age of Mythology," set up in my mind a chain of thought later leading to the conception of a large part of the present work.

To two of my colleagues, Professor Robert M. Brown and Professor Clayton H. Charles, I am under very deep obligations. Without their assistance I could not have written the chapter dealing with modern music and painting. Their help was essential, but they are not to be held responsible for the conclusions I draw nor for the accuracy of all the information I adduce.

I cannot forbear taking this opportunity to express my gratitude to John B. Chambers and Dudley Zuver, of the Harper editorial staff, who have taken an interest that is far more than professional in this book, and have aided me more than they can realize in the successive revisions of the manuscript.

Most of all I am indebted to my wife, Eva, who has helped me by her discerning criticism of both the style and the ideas of the book. She has encouraged me to think out the full consequences of a Christian viewpoint more thoroughly than I would otherwise have done. Many passages are echoes of our conversations, and her name would appear on the title page as co-author if she had not sternly forbidden me this pleasure.

CHAD WALSH

Beloit College
October, 1949

PART ONE

This Is the Way the World Ends

1

The Age of Mythology

The history of China has moved in cycles. At the beginning of the cycle we see a strong emperor sitting on the throne; in him is invested the "Mandate of Heaven," by virtue of which he reigns over the entire empire, maintaining justice and protecting the land from domestic tumult and foreign invasion. In time, his successors prove less competent. The central government weakens. The war lords of the provinces grow bolder and tentatively test the emperor's power. Finding it inadequate to strike back, they assume more and more powers to themselves, until the national regime becomes a futile shadow and the Mandate of Heaven drops from the emperor's shoulders.

China then turns into a conglomeration of provinces, each ruled over by a war lord, each frequently at war with the others. The patient people carry on, grateful that their regional masters at least maintain a semblance of order and keep the bandits under control. But all the while, a racial memory of the emperor and his Mandate of Heaven hovers in the consciousness of the nation; the period of disintegration is something to be lived through, not an end in itself.

That is one half of the cycle. The other is the re-establishment of the Mandate of Heaven. In a couple of cases it has come through a foreign invasion, when the leader of the invaders set himself upon the imperial throne and reknit the nation into one unit. More often, a provincial war lord has arisen, stronger than his rivals, and finally gained complete control of the country by reducing the other war lords to their proper position of subordination. Thereupon, the Mandate of Heaven descends upon the shoulders of the new emperor, and the life of the nation regains its old integration, every aspect being in proper balance.

China in its times of disorder and disunity is a fitting symbol of Western civilization today. There is no center to anything; the provinces of human life exercise complete home rule, each under its particular war lord and tyrant.

This is most obvious in the class struggle. Labor and capital snarl at each other across the conference table or the picket line; the farmer snarls at both. Only in time of war is an approximation of national unity achieved, and that rests upon a larger clash of provinces: one nation against another.

Everywhere one looks, the splitting up into provinces can be seen. Education has gone cafeteria-style because no one has any very clear idea of what education is. Art tends to drift off into "art for art's sake," and becomes more and more irrelevant to everything else. Within the individual, the provinces of his personality fall apart, until he is by turn half-a-dozen people: a tender father and husband at breakfast, a predatory businessman at the office, a sentimental backslapper at the Rotary Club, a dilettante at the concert, and a Christian for one hour a week on Sunday morning.

I suppose that no period of history has achieved complete integration, but some periods have come much closer to it than ours. During the Middle Ages, Christianity was the

Mandate of Heaven; it shaped education, inspired art, regulated family life, and had much to say about the economic relationships of men with one another (for example, the prohibition of usury). I am far from setting up the Middle Ages as a period to be slavishly imitated—it was a curious blend of holiness and nastiness—but the degree of integration created then is encouraging evidence that the social and psychological fragmentation of today is not necessarily permanent.

The reuniting of the rebel provinces of society and the individual's soul—and that is what the creation of a new civilization will essentially consist of—is rendered more difficult by the gradual development of a new picture of human nature—a picture faithfully reflecting the prevailing fragmentation. The more firmly the new picture becomes embedded in popular thinking, the more it will seem the expression of eternal reality rather than merely a reflection of the human soul in a very troubled and peculiar period of history.

This brings us to the Age of Mythology. A myth, of course, is not a myth until you have stopped believing in it. The little boy in a country village does not have a mythology when he searches for hobgoblins on Halloween night or listens on Christmas Eve for the harness bells of Santa's sleigh. He is merely acting as would any sensible adult who shared his knowledge of reality. The folklore of childhood fades easily, almost painlessly, into mythology. Daddy is detected filling the stockings by the fireplace, and that is the end of Santa Claus. The traveling salesman jeers the hobgoblins away.

Once a myth is called a myth, it loses its power to harm, and sometimes it proves useful as a kind of linguistic shorthand. The young man who no longer believes in Santa

Claus can still say of a generous friend, "He is a perfect Santa Claus to everyone he knows." But the enlightened man will never hang up his stocking in an empty house and be disappointed to find it unfilled on Christmas morning.

The age-old mythology of the village store and the village child quickly vanishes; indeed, it is rapidly becoming extinct even among small children. But this does not mean that mythology is a thing of the benighted past. Old myths are simply replaced by new ones, and the new ones are believed by adults as well as children.

The new mythology is ingratiatingly adapted to the modern taste. It says nothing about gods and goddesses, ghosts and evil spirits. It deals with man. And it goes by any name but mythology. It is the New Thought, the Modern Way of Looking at Things, the Forward View. It is the joint creation of many minds—professors, writers, lecturers. It is disseminated by bright young instructors in the classroom and by the still brighter young men who pick up scraps of advanced learning and write articles for the Sunday supplements. They offer us—and we gratefully accept—four dominant myths: Economic Man, Biological Man, Environmental Man, and Psychoanalytic Man.

Economic Man is the easiest to portray. He is out to get anything that is not nailed down. Assassinating a rival or starting a world war is all in the day's business. But, unlike the traditional miser, he does not acquire money for the sake of hoarding it under his pillow. He gets it in order to turn it into more money, and so on, ad infinitum.

Ever since the discovery of Economic Man he has enjoyed a phenomenal vogue. It is true that the experts have differed in their evaluation of him, one school believing that if only he would be sufficiently self-centered the earth would automatically be converted into paradise, and a more recent school considering him the devil incarnate and a fit candidate for liquidation. However, these are minor controversies within the general faith.

If we were dealing only with the past, it would do no great harm to see in every Tom, Dick, and Harry a replica of Economic Man. The past is blissfully over and done with. Unhappily, the doctrine of Economic Man has been seized upon as a crystal ball. When Chamberlain met with another statesman at Munich and brought peace in our time at the expense of a nation too remote to matter, he was no doubt thinking to himself: "Germany is behaving like sixty million normal Economic Men; give her a good chunk of Czecho-slovakia and her appetite will be satisfied for our time." Had Chamberlain been right in his analysis, the cities of Europe would not resemble abandoned quarries today. As it happened, he was wrong. Germany was not a go-getter businessman. The land of Hitler and Himmler was wild-eyed with missionary zeal to spread Kultur by fire, sword, and dive bomber.

The average man, being less naïve than his leaders, finds occasionally that Economic Man does not explain everything. There is the strange conduct of the millionaire's son. The young fellow perversely marries a penniless chorus girl instead of an heiress.

The modern mythology-that-isn't-called-a-mythology has an explanation handy. It retreats to its second line of defense and whistles for Biological Man.

The great value of Biological Man is that he is permitted a sex life. Economic man may have greater prestige in graduate schools, but Biological Man is closer to the hearts of the people and the talents of scenario writers. However, we have not yet banished all mysteries from humanity. There is the case of the man who could have grown rich

manufacturing juke boxes, but who chooses instead to become a violinist at one-twentieth the income that might
have been his. How to explain his irrational behavior?

Clearly, he is not Economic Man; he has embraced
poverty instead of riches. He can scarcely be Biological
Man, for no scientist has posited a close connection between
physical urges and the technique of the violin. It is at this
point that modern thought makes a strategic retreat to the
third line of defense and radios an urgent appeal to Environmental Man.

Environmental Man comes trotting on the scene, his
pockets bulging with treatises on group adjustment and
social patterns. When interviewed, he patiently explains
that the man who unreasonably decided to become a violinist must have been conditioned by early experiences. Perhaps some one in his family owned a phonograph or radio
and he listened to violin music at a susceptible moment in
his life. At the very least, he once saw a picture of a violin
in a Sears Roebuck catalogue. Certainly he did not make
the decision of his own free will, for the books (here Environmental Man turns to a dog-eared page) state clearly
that he does not have any. The decision was made for him
very likely by circumstances that seemed so insignificant at
the time that the best hypnotist would probe the man's
memory in vain.

It is a watertight theory. It is based on an act of faith
which has nothing to do with scientific experimentation and
proof. The act of faith is an eternal *if*. *If* we knew literally
everything about a person's background and experiences,
we should be able not only to explain all his actions but
also to predict what he will do next. The *if* is a manifest
impossibility. A rich man might endow a talkie cameraman
to pursue a baby from the cradle to the grave, but the

photographer would doubtless pause to light a cigarette at the crucial moment when the child, aged three years, seven months, two days, six hours, seventeen minutes, and four seconds, saw his father pull a beer bottle out of the frigidaire; and from that moment the child would be conditioned to set up business in Milwaukee.

We have not yet reached the innermost citadel of the modern mythology. If someone points out the obvious fact that two children in a family, both having had essentially the same experiences—eating the same food, studying under the same teachers, learning the same platitudes at their mother's knee—turn out very differently, one becoming a pickpocket and the other a professor of biochemistry, and that it seems improbable any subtle differences in experience can account for these divergent careers, a deus ex machina is lugged on to the stage. Psychoanalytic Man (the great escape clause of the modern mythology) makes his bow.

Of the Mythological Men, only Psychoanalytic Man is free to behave in a way that seems completely mad to the naked eye. He can do so because his impulses arise from the uncharted depths of the subconscious. If I scream at the sight of table napkins, it can be proved that my motives are indisputably psychoanalytic. The reasoning is a simple process of elimination: (1) I gain nothing financially by screaming at the napkin. If I were Economic Man, I would steal it or buy it and sell it for a fancy price on the black market. (2) Napkins neither aid nor hinder the expression of the biological drives. (3) Nothing can be found or imagined in my background to suggest any unusual experiences with napkins. (4) Therefore, all other explanations having been tried and found wanting, my horror of napkins arises from the depths of my subconscious. *Q.E.D.*

Before proceeding to detail the practical consequences of the modern mythology, the devil should be given his due. A mythology, as I have said, is not harmful in itself, *provided that it is recognized for what it is.* The four great myths correspond to four of the rebellious provinces of human life, and to that extent they are descriptively accurate. If we do not endeavor to explain everything by them, we can explain—or at least symbolize—a great deal. Just as the Santa Claus myth furnishes a handy way of describing a generous man, we could speak of Economic Man and merely point out that nearly everyone has some lust for gain. Biological Man is another good shorthand symbol. It helps to shield us from the illusion that we are disembodied spirits; it reminds us that we are also eating, drinking, and breeding animals. Environmental Man drives home the fact that a child brought up among racketeers is likely (though not certain) to become a racketeer, and that, therefore, society should work to create an environment which will not expose children to excessively strong temptations. The wildest symbol of all, Psychoanalytic Man, is the most valuable. It reminds us of how little we still know about the murky depths of human nature, and how superficial is the rationalist delusion that all human difficulties can be solved like problems in trigonometry.

But the rebellious provinces number more than four. Once we admit that we are dealing with shorthand-myths, we need to enrich our mythology. We must make room for the Man of Pride, who lives to be admired; and the Man of Power, who scorns money as such and lives only in order to dominate. There is also Patriotic Man, who—rightly or wrongly—puts his nation ahead of himself. We must reserve a niche for Esthetic Man, and, strange as it sounds, we need also to reckon with Ethical Man, whose life is hag-

ridden by a sense of right and wrong that often runs counter
to the shrewd teachings of his parents. These additions are
only the most obvious ones; a whole generation of myth-
makers would have to labor at the creation of an adequate
gallery of myths.

Last—and most important—we should have to include
X-Man, to suggest the unknown quantity in every man—
the unpredictable corner of his being which laughs at all
conditioning influences. Here free will sits enthroned and
makes decisions.

All this is an excursion into utopian musing. I see no clear
signs that either the masses or the classes in America are
ready to examine their unrecognized mythology with the
same candid scrutiny they direct against the folklore of
children and country yokels. The schools and colleges,
swarming with record enrollments, are laboring earnestly
to graduate a bumper crop of young men and women who
are incapable of identifying a myth when they see one.

The newer, abundantly footnoted myths bode us more
harm than all the bad fairies and ghosts of the Dark Ages.
The average man, moving in the course of a single day
through one province of life after another, vaguely yearns
for a glimpse of an over-all pattern or meaning to his existence. He wants to feel that his business life, his family life,
his club life, and all his other lives are somehow connected,
and that his life as a whole is not a series of disconnected
fragments. He wants to know what the purpose of life is.
But the modern mythology gives him no help. It shoves
him back into the four rebellious provinces, one after the
other, and while he is in one province he is prevented from
communicating with the others. When he occasionally ventures into one of the unrecognized provinces (such as art
or religion) he is made to feel that he is in a land of com-

plete unreality, because no standard label has been provided for it. Meanwhile he grows old, and death is waiting
to conquer all the familiar provinces.

It may seem that I have fantastically exaggerated the
practical importance of the national faith in the four myths.
"After all, it isn't what a man believes, but what he does,
that matters." But what a man does is often the result of
what he believes. Hitler's crusade against civilization was
the practical expression of the philosophy expounded in
Mein Kampf; the Communist Revolution in Russia was
preceded by *The Communist Manifesto*. The pen is mightier
than the sword because the soldier executes what the philosopher proposes.

The greatest importance of the modern mythology is that
all four myths are subdivisions of the one supreme myth:
Irresponsible Man. And a devout faith in the latter strips
the believers of the three attributes that separate them from
the beasts of the field.

The first attribute to go is free will. Each of us, according
to the mythology-that-isn't-called-a-mythology, is a walking
machine. We respond now to greed, now to biological urges,
now to environmental conditioning, now to the irrational
promptings of the subconscious. In no case do we have any
say in the matter. Unseeing forces pull the levers; we obey.
Doomed to do this or that by senseless forces, we can
neither curse nor glorify the agents of our destiny. They
are impersonal; they do not understand the English language or any language. One does not erect altars to economic determinism, invoke it in prayer, or stick pins in wax
images of it.

The destruction of faith in free will entails an ironic
paradox. The doctrine of predestination, long loathed by
advanced thinkers as a hideous Calvinistic abomination, has

reappeared, clothed in the latest fashions, and now dominates the thought of the age more tyrannically than during Calvin's days at Geneva. The new predestination is acceptable to the sophisticated and enlightened because it is not called predestination. But to a man in a strait jacket it is of small importance whether God or a blindfolded "force" draws the laces together.

Free will flies out the window, and with it morality departs. Words like "just," "unjust," "right," and "wrong" become mere words once the possibility of making decisions is ruled out. You deserve no credit for helping an old lady across the intersection and no blame for mismanaging her savings. Blind forces, not you, made the decision in either case.

The next step—a very easy and consoling one—is to say that what you are conditioned to do doesn't really matter anyhow. "It all depends on the way you look at it." Ideas of right and wrong do not drift down to us from God, nor do they frolic as absolutes in the realm of platonic metaphysics. Like a sudden impulse to scratch one's nose, they are mechanical responses to stimuli that have never heard of the Ten Commandments.

Here we encounter another paradox. A new kind of hypocrisy has arisen. Instead of preaching good and practicing evil, the new hypocrite asserts that there is no such thing as good or evil and then acts as though every word he has spoken was a lie. The result is a split personality. It can be seen, for example, in teachers who have learned both behavioristic psychology and "social-mindedness" in the schools of education. Armed with teaching certificates, they go forth to inculcate one-world-mindedness and many other admirable attitudes in their students, and at the same time they devoutly believe (because their professors have told them so) that everything anyone does is predetermined. Why the fine moral fervor? If belief in one-world-mindedness is the by-product of chance influences, then the views of the *Chicago Tribune* are as valid as those of the *Washington Post*.

The same split personality is found in reformers who have been exposed to the modern enlightenment. In them, too, the right lobe of the brain never knows what the left lobe is thinking. One side of the brain is stuffed with the doctrines of the new predestination; the other is a filing case of plans for a brave new world—plans that could never have been conceived and could not possibly be translated into community nurseries and group housing projects, unless somebody along the way had gained some inkling of the nature of a *good* society, and had freely used his brains to make plans.

Eventually the left lobe and the right lobe will compare notes, and the split personality will come out into the open. When that happens the split must be healed. This can be done in one of two ways. The most obvious is to accept the new predestination so devoutly that it becomes true. There are great advantages to this solution. It offers as its reward the all-inclusive alibi: "Don't blame me, don't blame anybody; forces beyond my control did it."

The enormous increase in the divorce rate during the past hundred years is the most striking example of healing the split by practicing what one preaches. In a subsequent chapter I shall have to deal with this in some detail, but for the moment I am concerned with the growing frequency of divorce only because it illustrates one way of curing the split personality. Popular opinion has gradually altered so that it seems reasonable for a wife to divorce her husband because he reads the evening paper at the dinner table, and for a husband to divorce his wife because she holds pins in her mouth. After all—it is reasoned—if they did not yield to impulse and go to Reno, they might develop serious neuroses; one mustn't resist the imperious forces of destiny. The same frame of mind can be applied to every human situation. The split personality is then healed: the new pre-destination becomes true—by a farewell act of free will. Men can turn themselves into machines if they try hard enough.

The other way of healing the split is to find logical reasons for believing in free will. To do so would be a drastic revo-lution in modern thought—so drastic that probably nothing short of a widespread religious conversion could bring it about. A discussion of this, however, must wait until Part Two.

I have not yet spoken of the third consequence of the modern mythology. That is the loss of any plausible basis for a belief in reason. If all my ideas are conditioned by forces that do not think, it seems logical to conclude that I cannot think. All ideas are accidental; one is as good as an-other. This simple deduction is recognized and exploited when expediency suggests it. In political arguments men shout at one another, "You believe in the Republican party because you never had to work with your hands"; or "You're a Democrat because you grew up in Alabama." If a man's opinions can be shown to be those we should expect from his background or experiences, we tranquilly assume that we have answered them.

The one citadel of reason (apart from theology) is the laboratory. There the scientist performs his experiments with as sturdy a faith in his own reasoning powers as Aristotle or Aquinas boasted. He believes that when he balances his equations they are really balanced, and that the mathematical statements in his notebook mean something.

It may be another twenty or thirty years before the citadel of science is stormed. Once the walls are breached, I can imagine the physics student saying to his professor: "I am quite willing to tolerate your ideas about gravitation, but surely you would not insist that I share them? Our backgrounds have been quite different. You have been conditioned by an early study of the works of Newton, and he in turn was doubtless conditioned by the absolutist theories of his age to believe that, because one apple chanced to fall to the ground, all apples had to fall." If the professor should mumble ancient phrases about experimental verification and the scientific method, the student would reasonably reply: "Who am I to trust the evidence of my eyes? Perhaps I think I see one apple, or many apples, fall to the ground, but everything the eye beholds must be interpreted by the brain, and the brain cannot think. It may be that the apples are really going up in the air—if there are such things as apples."

But this is getting ahead of current history. We still live in a blurred, inconsistent period, with free will and its fellow travelers, morality and reason, largely banished from theorizings about human nature, though practiced secretly in the laboratories. And all the while, the metaphysics of our unrecognized mythology exerts a steady tug. Day by day we are thrust more firmly into the rebellious provinces, first into one and then into another. If we do not revolt and go on some exploring expeditions of our own, we shall advance ever closer to the moment when the desire to revolt is dead and the age of the walking machines is ready to begin.

2

Creative Rats and the Sinking Ship

If it is true that life has split up into a large number of self-sufficient provinces, each of which claims to be the whole of reality, it comes as no surprise to find the arts constituting one province. The doctrine of "art for art's sake," though not universally held, is still the subconscious assumption of most creative workers, and the more thoroughly they live by it the more effectively they isolate their province from all other provinces.

I am not concerned here with the question of whether "art for art's sake" is esthetically tenable. I am not thinking of esthetics at all. Perhaps Picasso and Joyce outrank Michelangelo and Homer, or the reverse may be the judgment of history. The question is one for students of esthetics to debate. What I should like to suggest is something else—that we can use writers, painters, and composers as barometers of deep-seated social and cultural changes—changes not yet obvious to the ordinary observer. The creative worker is typically a person with abnormal sensitivity to the invisible vibrations in the atmosphere; like a dog, he can hear sounds too high for ordinary ears. If the fragmentation of society and the individual's soul has actually taken place, we should expect to find it reflected in the arts. I think we do.

Consider painting first. The changes in the past half century have been so astonishing that the most obtuse Philistine is painfully aware of them. If you go to any museum of modern art and listen to the visitors as they pause first in front of a good specimen of cubist art (say the torso of a trout reduced to the austere lines of geometry) and then linger briefly before one of Dali's wilder fancies, you will discover bewilderment strongly blended with indignation.

The average citizen, the much-deplored Philistine, has been bullheaded and conservative during all periods of history. He has hooted at Whistler's "The Artist's Mother," and his grandsons have hooted at Picasso's "Guernica." But, in defense of the modern Philistine, it must be admitted that his nervous system has been subjected to a series of severe shocks. Never has the gap between popular taste and the works of the *avant-garde* been as great as in the past fifty years. The changes in art during that time are more sweeping than during the whole century preceding.

The Philistine, loathing what he sees before him, dismisses modern art with a contemptuous "Those artists are crazy, all of 'em." But there is another possible explanation. Perhaps the artist is exceptionally sane or at least gifted with unusually keen eyes. Modern art may mirror a basic breakdown of society and civilization—mirror it and to some extent foretell the stages yet to come. The familiar traffic lights still function in America, and no rubble obstructs the streets, but the physical monuments of a civilization can remain in good preservation after its inner core has withered away.

If modern art is actually an obituary (and perhaps also a prophesy of things to come), it is interesting to discover when the danger signals first began flying. The impressionist movement in the second half of the last century seems the best starting point. It marks the transition between the realism of Renaissance art and the subjectivism of modern art. To put it simply—too simply—painting had for several centuries been largely photographic; the artist had endeavored to depict people, buildings, trees, and skies in such a way that they would be recognized by visitors to the art gallery. Impressionism was the culmination of photographic realism and the beginning of its downfall. To the impressionist, all things were in a state of flux. The duty of the artist was to record the scene as the light waves struck his eyes at 3:17 P.M. of a slightly overcast day in late August. To him there was no such thing as a "house" per se; there was only the impression that something conveniently called a house happened to make on his optic nerves at a particular moment. Next day, or next hour, the lighting conditions might have changed so greatly that the "house" would appear on the second canvas as a structure having little recognizable resemblance to the first one.

Impressionism developed in the nineteenth century, an age loath to acknowledge any kind of reality that you cannot stub your toe against. One consequence was that the portraits painted by the impressionists were almost invariably unsatisfactory. To a logical impressionist, a cabbage was as interesting as a king, and the same technique would do for both. In his picture, "Execution of Emperor Maximilian," Édouard Manet did not trouble to show the emperor's face—it is hidden by the smoke from the rifles. Nor are the faces of the riflemen individualized; they are as void of human traits as a cluster of poplar trees. The points of emphasis are white headdresses, gaiters, belts—things that would strike the eyes first if the observer took no interest in the purpose of this strange meeting. The painting shows "scientific objectivity" carried over into the realm of brush and canvas.

In impressionism the artist painted the scene as it struck

his eyes; the resulting picture was a subjective rendering of an objective reality. In post-impressionism and expressionism the artist plunges much further into subjectivism. The concrete world becomes the raw material for expressing the feelings seething inside him. Van Gogh's "Cornfield with Cypresses" says less about cornfields than the passions of Van Gogh.

Expressionism was succeeded by a procession of schools, none of which completely dominated painting at any time and many of which chronologically overlapped. Today it is almost impossible to discern any main trends: every artist is a law unto himself. But almost all modern artists agree in joyfully accepting the freedom won for them by expressionism. The artist is no longer obliged to be a camera.

Of the schools of painting that have followed expressionism in such profusion, abstract art and surrealism are surely the most astonishing. Abstract art does not pretend to present even a distorted image of the phenomenal world. Its figures are symbols, meaningful to the artist but frequently merely mystifying to the spectator. The ambiguity of abstract art is what separates it from the symbolism of medieval art. The artist of the Middle Ages painted pictures that symbolized the beliefs most people held in common. There was a community of beliefs and a recognized set of symbols: a halo for holiness, etc. Today both a set of common beliefs and a set of common symbols are lacking; the artist creates private symbols for private concepts.

Surrealism is an equally emphatic defiance of photography. Nightmare forms, projections of the subconscious, dissected fragments of the visible world—all are rearranged and thrown together. And it is exactly this quality—its close ties with the subconscious—that makes surrealism so disquieting a commentary on present-day civilization. One stares with honest loathing at Dali's "Soft Construction with Boiled Beans; Premonition of Civil War," but uneasy thoughts punctuate the loathing. Who is crazy? Is it Dali? It would be comfortable to think so. But perhaps that giant hand he has painted, holding aloft a distorted torso on which reposes a savage head with buck-teeth and long locks, is not the insane daub of someone who should be institutionalized. The horror that will not let you leave it may spring from your unconscious awareness that Dali has passed beyond photographic realism to psychic realism and has painted a portrait of the soul of twentieth-century man.

I cannot escape the feeling that modern artists are doing more than mirroring the inner collapse of a culture. By the very act of revolting against the literal and meaningless fact, they show themselves hungry for meaning behind the fact. They know, as medieval man did, that a tree or a house by itself means nothing; that there must be something beyond the things perceived by the senses for material objects to make sense. Perhaps most artists are now wandering in the wasteland of meaninglessness, but that does not mean they like it there. They are feeling their way through it, hoping to find meaning on the other side.

The innovations in modern music have been less sweeping than those in painting. The reason may well be that music already enjoyed a freedom for which painting had to wage a savage struggle: freedom from the tyranny of the external world. For centuries the painter was expected to be a gifted camera, but the composer was not asked (except for special purposes) to reproduce the braying of asses or the twitter of birds.

However, there are suggestive parallels between modern painting and modern music. The surrealist painter disintegrates the visible world; the ultramodern composer disintegrates the long-established system of keys and scales. Beginning with Debussy who popularized—if he he did not invent—the whole tone scale, and going on to the radical experiments of Arnold Schönberg and his twelve-tone system of harmony, the old distinction between consonance and dissonance has become increasingly obscured, and tonality less obvious.

In such a work as Schönberg's *Pierrot Lunaire* (by no means the most advanced of his experiments), the result is a fascinating but singularly frustrating inconclusiveness. One feels plunged into a world where nothing begins and nothing can conceivably cease. For a moment a small island of stability will be created, but it is soon swept away into the flux of sound.

Schönberg and his school are admittedly extreme examples of modern music, but the tendencies they represent are found in milder form in many composers. Any musician who had flourished between 1750 and 1850 would find himself hurled into a new musical "frame of reference" could he enter a modern concert hall.

Easier for the layman to recognize and analyze are the modern developments in literature, especially poetry. Here again the nineteenth century is the great watershed. The poetic technique of Shakespeare and Keats was not so dissimilar but that each would have understood what the other was attempting. Both made abundant use of rhyme, except when they turned to blank verse with its sober norm of iambic pentameter. Shakespeare might have been glad to claim "The Eve of St. Agnes" as his own; many of Keats' sonnets would not sound out of place in a collected *Shakespeare*.

Walt Whitman was the most conspicuous pioneer of modern poetry in the English-speaking world. He overthrew

the domination of rhyme, and—much more drastic deed—
he shattered the conventional analyses of rhythm. The
school "marm," trained to look for iambs, trochees, ana-
paests, and dactyls, plus lines containing a definite number
of feet, stood appalled before:

> I celebrate myself, and sing myself,
> And what I assume you shall assume,
> For every atom belonging to me as good belongs to you.
>
> I loafe and invite my soul,
> I learn and loafe at my ease observing a spear of
>   summer grass.
>
> My tongue, every atom of my blood, form'd from this
>   soil, this air,
> Born here of parents born here from parents the same,
>   and their parents the same,
> I, now thirty-seven years old in perfect health begin,
> Hoping to cease not till death.

The first line trots along in reassuringly strict blank verse;
with the second, chaos breaks loose. This strange new
rhythm cannot be reduced to a tidy diagram on the black-
board.

The rhythms of Whitman are echoed and elaborated in
the poetry of Carl Sandburg and the host of other free-
versifiers who burst into prominence around the time of
World War I. But their revolution was yet a mild one. They
revolutionized English versification but not the structure of
the English language.

With such a poet as E. E. Cummings, syntax and the word
itself are subjected to strange surgery. Words are hacked
into pieces like the fragments in a surrealist picture. The
effect is strangely meaningful at its best, but the meaning

defies ready analysis. For a relatively conservative example,
take "Poem 279" in W:[1]

> Do.
> omful
> relaxing
>
> -ly)i
> downrise outwrithein-
> ing upfall and
>
> Am the glad deep the living from nowh
> -ere(!firm!)exp-
> anding,am a fe
>
> -rvently(susta-
> inin
> -gness Am
>
> root air rock day)
> :you;
> smile,hands
>
> (an-
> onymo
> -Us

A similar disintegration of syntax can be seen in much of
Gertrude Stein's prose. "A rose is a rose is a rose" is not the
most advanced of her linguistic experiments. The complete
transformation of both syntax and the word is reached in
James Joyce's *Ulysses* and *Finnegans Wake*. His method
can be seen in the first two paragraphs of the latter:[2]

[1] E. E. Cummings, *Collected Poems* (New York: Harcourt, Brace
& Co., 1944). Copyright, 1935, by E. E. Cummings. Quoted by
permission of the publisher.
[2] *Finnegans Wake* (New York: The Viking Press, 1944), p. 3.
Quoted by permission of the publishers.

riverrun, past Eve and Adam's, from swerve of shore to bend of bay, brings us by a commodius vicus of recirculation back to Howth Castle and Environs.

Sir Tristrem, violer d'amores, fr'over the short sea, had passencore rearrived from North Amorica on this side the scraggy isthmus of Europe Minor to wielderfight his penisolate war: nor had topsawyer's rocks by the stream Oconee exaggerated themselse to Laurens County's gorgios while they went doublin their mumper all the time: nor avoice from afire bellowsed mishe mishe to tauf tauf thuartpeatrick: not yet, though venissoon after, had a kidscad buttended a bland old isaac: not yet, though all's fair in vanessy, were sosie sesthers wroth with twone nathandjoe. Rot a peck of pa's malt had Jhem or Shen brewed by arclight and rory end to the regginbrow was to be seen ringsome on the aquaface.

It may be objected that I have singled out the most extreme examples of modern writing. And so I have. I have done the same thing with painting and music, for that matter. The more extreme the examples, the clearer the implications.

It is quite true that few writers have carried linguistic disintegration as far as E. E. Cummings and James Joyce. Language is, after all, primarily an instrument of thought. If one wishes to convey an overpowering emotion, language may be able to do it; but there is always the risk that some *thoughts* will get mixed in with the emotion. Painting and music, not being used as everyday means of ordering a cup of coffee or discussing politics, can be handled with more freedom, and are better suited for expressing chemically pure emotions.

This brings up a hopeful possibility. Writers, being obliged to wrestle with words, are perhaps driven to *think* whether they want to or not. We might therefore plausibly expect the first glimmerings of a new civilization to appear in literature before they are discernible in other arts. I fancy this is already the case. Among the "post-modern" writers I would include two of the most distinguished poets now living in the English-speaking world: T. S. Eliot and W. H. Auden. In their technique they have assimilated everything the experimenters have developed, but one reads their books with a feeling that they have gone beyond change for change's sake, that they, in both technique and ideas, have worked their way through to a land still terra incognita to most of us. Their feet seem to be on solid ground once more.

Traces of "post-modern" painting are also beginning to be evident. Among the best present-day artists there is no tendency to return to the good old days before impressionism. Rather, the aim is the same as that of the most significant modern poets: to pass through the confusion, assimilating any of its useful techniques, and re-establish contact with the public after reaching the other side of the morass. An excellent example is the British sculptor and artist, Henry Moore. His work would not be what it is if Picasso and Epstein had not come before him, but he is not content to remain in a period of perpetual experiment-for-experiment's-sake. His abstractions show signs of taking on public meaning; some of his paintings, such as the air-raid-shelter scenes, are as hauntingly symbolic as the art of the early Middle Ages; his highly stylized statue of the three listening women recently won the favorable attention of many erstwhile Philistines when it was displayed in London. He, and some others like him, are gradually making contact with the public—but by going forward, not backward.

However, the Eliots, Audens, and Moores are still few in number. Taking the twentieth-century arts as a whole, the impression is overwhelming that they mirror an inner collapse of society. The breakdown of the familiar system of tonality and harmony in music; the amazing shift from photographic art to the art of subjective symbolism; the advances of free verse, dissected words, and syntaxless grammar—all add up to a strong suggestion that civilization as Queen Victoria knew it is mutating into something unpredictable but different.

The developments in the arts strikingly parallel the rise of the modern mythology. Surrealist art, with its disquieting use of fragments from outer reality, must have underground connections with the idea of Psychoanalytic Man. Impressionism, dutifully depicting the impinging of light waves, suggests Environmental Man. I suspect that similar connections could be found between other esthetic developments and the modern concepts of human nature. In both realms what we find are various sorts of fragmentation.

However, I concede that the attempt to show a close relationship between what is happening to art and what is happening to civilization cannot be entirely convincing to the skeptic. There are too many subjective factors involved. To avoid becoming entangled in endless and controversial details, it is best to retreat to the bald statement which both the art critic and the Philistine will support: *Literature, painting, and music have changed much more from 1850 to today than they changed from 1750 to 1850.*

Can it be shown that the arts in the past have changed rapidly when one type of civilization was being replaced by another? Our ignorance of certain periods makes absolute certainty difficult (for example, we know very little of Greco-Roman music), but there is an impressive amount of evidence pointing in this direction.

For the sake of discussion—though with inevitable oversimplification—we can divide European history into "periods." The Christianization of the Mediterranean world, coupled with the fall of the Roman Empire in the fifth century A.D., marked the end of *Classical* civilization. This was followed by a *Christian* civilization, which developed through the Dark Ages and reached its zenith in the Middle Ages. The Middle Ages came to an end with the Renaissance of the fourteenth to sixteenth centuries, and *modern* civilization was ushered in. (In this scheme of classification, the Renaissance is not so much a period in itself as a time of transition.)

The shift from classical civilization to early Christian civilization was accompanied by conspicuous changes in poetry. Ancient Greek poetry (dutifully imitated by the Romans) was quantitative: the rhythm was determined not by a contrast between stressed and unstressed syllables but by the length of time ("short" or "long") required to pronounce a given syllable. The system began to break down in the fifth century. The "Pervigilium Veneris," a long poem usually attributed to that century, shows clear signs of the shift to qualitative versification—a dependence on stressed and unstressed syllables for rhythm. Versification of this sort had probably had a humble existence on the popular level for some time before classical civilization cracked up, but once the crash came it soon began to dominate both the secular and sacred poetry of the age.

This was not the only change. Rhyme, which had been an incidental ornament of classical verse, became almost the main technical characteristic of poetry. The lines tended to become much shorter than the stately and long-winded hexameter. In other words, medieval Latin poetry was essentially the same in technique as that familiar to the English-speaking world before the advent of Walt Whitman.

The replacement of classical versification by the newer models was a literary revolution almost as drastic as the onslaught of free verse in modern times. But it was not merely poetry that evolved into new forms. Painting, which had dealt realistically with the human body, became symbolical and culminated in the otherworldly strangeness of Byzantine religious art, which was not meant to show men as the camera sees them but to suggest certain religious truths about them and through them.

The Renaissance—that ill-defined frontier between the Middle Ages and the Modern period—reached England in full force during the sixteenth century. A few gallant but hopeless attempts were made to impose classical quantitative versification on English poetry, but a more modest revolution was effected. The sonnet—a lyric form incomparable for compactness and balanced proportions—was introduced into English poetry, and at about the same time blank verse made its debut, thus ending the long bondage to compulsory rhyme.

The paintings and statues of the Renaissance everywhere reveal so obvious a change in spirit that they scarcely demand comment. They represent an intentional return to classical standards, a concentration on man as such and beauty of form for its own sake. The patronage of the arts passed more and more into the hands of the nobility, and secular subjects became favored over religious ones.

Religious art, of course, did not die out, but its spirit was subtly altered. One can sense the change by comparing "The Visitation" of Albertinelli (1474-1515) and "The Mystic Marriage of St. Catherine" by Correggio (1494-1534). The former shows the painstaking Renaissance respect for technical exactitude, but there is something quietly medieval about the position of Mary and Elizabeth as they lean toward each other. At their meeting a mystery is being communicated. Their faces are so shaded that the two women seem less individual beings than symbols of the miraculous life within them.

In "The Mystic Marriage," religious art is well on the way to the debased, sentimental pictures of Sunday-school leaflets. The Christ child is "cute"—there is no other word for it—and the three adults around Him look like the doting elders of any period; St. Catherine herself seems on the point of tickling the infant's toes. One senses that the artist would have preferred to paint princesses, Venus, and shepherd girls, but—since the public still demanded religious art—he was determined to prettify and demysticize it as much as possible.

But this is enough of enumerations. All I want to suggest is that the end of classical civilization and the end of the Middle Ages were accompanied by extensive changes in the arts. The past hundred years of our period have seen changes at least as violent. Whatever conclusions are drawn from this will tend, I think, to confirm the evidence afforded by the modern mythology that basic cultural changes are taking place—changes too deep-seated and all-embracing for us, who are in their midst, fully to comprehend. It is uncomfortable to face the new and unpredictable, but that seems to be the destiny of all of us now living.

Endings and Beginnings

If our present civilization is dying, what sort of civilization is it? It is precisely at this point that the Christian and the secularist draw opposite conclusions. The secularist points out reasonably enough that from the days of the apostles down to fairly recent times Christianity was on the march. By persuasion, palace intrigues, and violence, it spread over most of Europe and then jumped the seas to the New World. Christianity has had many centuries in which to demonstrate its worth—and has failed. Because it has failed, people are turning away from it. The Christian Era is drawing to a close. Once it is thoroughly dead and men have ridded themselves of its archaic superstitions, humanity will move forward to unimaginable heights of progress.

To this the Christian replies that the civilization now in its death agonies is not Christian. Or, to put it more exactly, it is only about 25 per cent Christian, and the Christian elements in it are largely unlabeled as such. (The modern jargon, with its "social consciousness" and the like, is an effective way of hiding the fact that the permanent values of secular idealism have been largely plagiarized from the Christian doctrines of the Fatherhood of God and the Brotherhood of Man.) Seventy-five per cent of present-day civilization is a murky blend of incredible optimism about

47

human nature (man is good and is getting better), super-
stitious faith that men will behave decently once they all
get a high school education, mystical trust in inevitable
progress, and—this above all—the passionate conviction
that science holds the key to utopia.

The impressive statistics of church membership should
deceive no one. The statistics are usually gathered in a
haphazard way that would appall a public accountant, and
desperate church officials have been known to indulge in
something remarkably like padding. Even if the figures
were all accurate, they would mean little. Many church
members never go to church, or only at Christmas and
Easter. Many who do go to church or say an occasional
private prayer are indulging in empty routine. Other Christians have relegated their religion to the compartment of
private piety and never take it out for an airing in the
market place. Or else they have remade it to fit the modern
temper. This latter is very easy to do. In many churches the
quality of Christianity has declined until there is little left
save the golden rule, a few moral injunctions, and vague
aspirations toward a well-integrated personality.

The decline in the total impact of Christianity began at
least as early as the eighteenth century. From the deism of
the eighteenth century to the agnosticism of the nineteenth
century to the confusion and demonic totalitarianism of the
twentieth century—one strand in all these developments is
the decline of Christianity: its abandonment by most intellectuals and its progressive dilution almost everywhere. Our
civilization is far more secular than Christian. And the
Christian commentator would add that it bids fair to be
short-lived: its dissolution is proceeding swiftly and vio-
lently.

We are the last scrawny descendants of the Renaissance.
The more one thinks about it, the more ambiguous that

period becomes. Perhaps Professor Sorokin's analysis is
helpful here. The Dark Ages and the early Middle Ages
were an *ideational* period—a time when concepts such as
God and the soul seemed more real than sticks and stones.
The late Middle Ages and the early Renaissance were an
idealistic period: the visible and invisible worlds were
equally balanced. The scales continued tipping, until now
the beam is almost vertical. Twentieth-century Europe and
America are as *sensate* as imperial Rome. History has come
full circle. The five senses are the touchstones of reality.

The real religion of our sensate period has been, logically
enough, a faith that might be equally well called materialism, or utopianism or scientism. In other words, the goal of
human life is plenty and comfort; science is the technique
for achieving the goal.

It is true that this quasi religion has recently been somewhat undermined by the two world wars and the shock
treatment administered by the totalitarian nations. It is
hard to be confident any more about the inevitability of
progress. The old materialist faith may still be strong with
the masses, but doubts are beginning to assail the more
thoughtful and alert segments of the population.

It is difficult to recall any civilization that has long sur-
vived and grown without a religious basis. And the religion
needs to be a real religion, with one or more gods or at least
a cosmic oversoul. The case of Confucianist China, often
cited in contradiction, is no exception. Confucianism may
be no more than a noble blend of etiquette, filial piety, and
civic righteousness (though some scholars would dispute
this), but the Chinese have never depended on Confucianism exclusively for any great length of time. They have
repeatedly reinforced it with the supernaturalism of Taoism
and Buddhism, and more recently with Christianity.

The history of Europe is even clearer. The Greeks and

Romans first worshiped the varied deities of Olympus, then largely forsook them for the strange divinities of the mystery cults, and finally turned to the strangest God of all—the one who stepped into history for the express purpose of dying a criminal's death. Occasional highbrows throughout history have made shift with mere philosophy, but the gods always return in the long run.

It may be objected that the future will not necessarily repeat the past. Civilizations up to the present have been associated with supernatural religion, but will this always be the case? Cannot we build a new civilization on a noble concept of man? What of humanism as the answer?

The questions are well put. The cyclic theories of history are too deterministic. Even granted that materialism and scientism are dime-store philosophies, based on an inadequate view of human possibilities, would it not be possible to found a civilization on a sober kind of humanism which dreamed not of technological utopias but of the fulfillment of man's highest nature?

I have great sympathy with the humanist. Next to theism, humanism is the loftiest outlook that anyone can have. It is much better to glorify man than a Diesel engine. Humanism also emphasizes the often forgotten fact that man and the beasts of the field, though biologically very similar, are otherwise extremely dissimilar: concertos, art museums, and systems of metaphysics are limited to humanity.

I admire humanism, but I do not believe it will work. In the first place, the humanist sets his sights too low. He takes for his model the highest kind of life that any mortal can live. That is too low a goal. Once in a generation there may be a St. Francis, a Jane Addams, an Albert Schweitzer, or a Gandhi, but these people—saints canonized or uncanonized—would be the first to protest in horror if they were held up as examples of perfection. In any event, there aren't enough of them to go around. Few of us ever have a chance to lay eyes on one saint, much less know him well enough to be personally inspired by him. The best that the average town can boast is a fair number of people who are reasonably decent to their neighbors and who, at irregular intervals, show real flashes of disinterested love and generosity. If the humanist chooses these local models for imitation his sights are set dangerously low, for when you imitate a model you always fall short of the original. The playwright who tries to be as great as Shakespeare will probably not succeed completely, but he will be a better writer than if he had merely tried to be as great as Maxwell Anderson.

Humanism, then, has no standard of absolute perfection. It has no God incarnate. It has only good and great men, and they are not enough. But the worst thing is this: Humanism still involves the old illusion of relying entirely on your own resources. The humanist cannot ask strength from anything or anybody greater and better than the best of men. God does not exist; therefore God cannot throw in the crucial extra ounce of strength.

In actual practice, humanism almost always evolves in one of two directions. Either the humanist becomes a collector of first editions, a Debussy faddist, a connoisseur of imported vintages—or he turns into a strong-armed do-gooder, eager to manipulate other people's lives.

I see no signs that humanism of the nobler kind will emerge full of vitality from the campuses and editorial offices where it largely dwells at present. However, there are other secular faiths of a more strident kind, and they are much in evidence. I have already spoken of scientism-materialism-utopianism, which is still probably the prevailing faith, though less vocal in high places than a few decades ago. Faiths of a more demanding sort have also sprung up and have inspired as much fanaticism as ever spurred the crusaders on to Jerusalem. Fascism is such a makeshift religion. By deifying the race it gave the individual something to believe in outside himself. Communism is another makeshift religion. It pushes to its logical extreme the cult of progress, and has for its god the classless society. But fascism, communism, ordinary materialism—all share the same defect. Like their noble cousin, humanism, they are wholly focused on this world. Directly or indirectly, the worshipers worship themselves.

The extreme cruelty and ruthlessness of recent history suggest that when man makes himself, his bosses, his society, or his race the measure of all things, he becomes less human rather than more. The other side of the paradox is more hopeful. When man makes something outside himself the measure of all things—when his absolute is God—he becomes more human as a by-product. God lifts him into genuine humanity.

This whole line of thought is frankly pragmatic. I am assuming that we want to be fully human, and that belief in God is the only force capable of making us human. In any event, there are a number of significant straws in the wind to indicate that the experiment in secularism is petering out. However, before discussing the evidence for this, I should like to speak of possible substitutes for secularism that do not involve the drastic alternative of Christianity.

Theoretically, the next religion might consist of the common features of the principal religions now existing. Mohammedanism, Christianity, and Judaism—to name only three—are all monotheistic, and have many moral teachings in common. The new religion could be monotheism combined with a simple code of morality.

Such a religion already exists in reality if not in name. It
is found in many of the more "modernist" Protestant
churches. Sometimes a conscious attempt is made to break
down any sharp distinction between Christianity and other
religions. For example, in some Unitarian churches passages
from the Talmud, the Koran, and the Sutras are read along
with the Bible. Modernist Christianity in general bears more
resemblance to liberal Judaism than to classical Christianity.

There is a great deal about such an attempt that commands respect if not assent. It is an honest endeavor to
concentrate on points of agreement in order to achieve wider
religious unity. But whatever the merits of the idea, it shows
little promise of success. The deity of the eclectic faith is
shadowy, and the moral code seldom more than a set of
vague generalities. There is little to grip either the heart
or the intellect. It is noticeable that the churches which have
gone the furthest toward eclectic vagueness are those with
the most listless members, whereas the churches—like the
Roman Catholic and Lutheran—which have retained classical Christianity with all its sharp edges are those that
inspire devotion in their members and mold their lives.

The best modern example of a forthright attempt to
found a world-religion on the common-denominator basis
is Bahai. It was established by its prophet Bahaullah around
the middle of the last century. Its founder deliberately
shaped it to include the best features of the religions with
which he was familiar. It is monotheistic; has a moral code
very similar to that of Christianity; teaches immortality.
Several of its doctrines make explicit the implications of
other religions and at the same time are calculated to
appeal to the modern idealist. Bahai emphasizes world
brotherhood, racial equality, the compatibility of science and
religion, the need for a world organization and a world

language. All in all, it strikingly resembles liberal Protestantism, and has the further advantage of being free of the unpleasant historical associations that cluster around almost all older religions. The Christian who honestly believes that all religions are basically similar and of equal worth could not do better than join the Bahai movement.

If a common-denominator religion is the wave of the future, Bahai ought to be sweeping all obstacles before it. It is not. Outside of its native Iran its progress has been very small, despite the genuine ardor and dedication of its followers. True, a century is not very long, but a third of a century was sufficient time for Christianity to become so obnoxious to the Romans that they singled it out for spectacular persecutions. Somehow Bahai has not caught on.

It is interesting to note in passing that even Bahai is not an absolutely pure example of monotheism-plus-morality. It has a few sharp edges. It has retained the Mohammedan prohibition of alcoholic beverages and it has established certain definite days for feasts and fasts. One suspects indeed that Bahai would spread faster if it acquired a few more sharp edges, such as a more definite type of religious service. One of the great appeals of early Christianity was the sharp distinction between the mores of Christians and those of the surrounding pagans.

Perhaps some religion of the Bahai type may yet appear and carry everything before it, but so far the indications are not encouraging. It is possible, however, that monotheism-plus-morality is not the only kind of common denominator. A small but very distinguished group of intellectuals has come forward in recent years with a different basis of agreement: mysticism.

This movement is an amazing thing to watch. In the very midst of a civilization intent on war, machines, money, and applied science, a number of the keenest minds of Europe and America have embraced "the perennial philosophy," "the eternal gospel"—or whatever other name is applied to it—and are conducting a frank missionary campaign to win converts. Two of Aldous Huxley's recent novels, *After Many a Summer Dies the Swan* and *Time Must Have a Stop,* are fictionized recruiting pamphlets. Christopher Isherwood has edited an anthology of Vedanta writings for occidental consumption. Gerald Heard, in addition to writing many books on mysticism, founded a small "college" (combination monastery-retreat) in California to train disciples in the technique of mysticism and investigate its psychology. Commercial publishing houses are bringing out many modern treatises on mysticism and reissuing the classical manuals.

Here we may have our fingers on a real wave of the future. Communism and Christianity, it will be remembered, were at first espoused by a handful of intense men. The literary and intellectual stature of the mystical missionaries is sufficient to demand thoughtful attention.

Huxley defines the perennial philosophy as "the metaphysic that recognizes a divine Reality substantial to the world of things and lives and minds; the psychology that finds in the soul something similar to, or even identical with, divine Reality; the ethic that places man's final end in the knowledge of the immanent and transcendent Ground of all being."[1] Like Gerald Heard, he regards mysticism as the highest common denominator of the great religions. At their heart is the belief that the individual can achieve spiritual communion and even union with the Godhead. All else—

[1] Aldous Huxley, *The Perennial Philosophy,* (New York): Harper & Brothers, 1945), p. vii. Quoted by permission of the publishers.

sacraments, priesthoods, feast days, fasts, elaborate theologies—are secondary trappings.

The other intellectual current that is flowing strongly among a small number of equally distinguished thinkers is Christianity—generally Christianity that is neither "modernist" nor "fundamentalist." It is classical Christianity—centered around the Incarnation and Atonement, but chary of excessive bibliolatry. G. K. Chesterton, before his death, was the most remarkable apologist for this central Christian tradition. Now that he is dead, the two most distinguished lay apologists are probably Dorothy Sayers and C. S. Lewis. And, as it was pointed out earlier, two of the most gifted poets in England and America are generally conceded to be T. S. Eliot and W. H. Auden, and both of them publicly advocate Christianity and make extensive use of Christian themes in their poetry.

If the intellectuals are really barometers of the future climate of opinion, the race seems to be between classical Christianity and a generalized form of mysticism. Which will win out? Perhaps both. When Christianity was at the height of its vigor, mysticism was one of its deepest resources. Only in the last few centuries has Christian mysticism tended to dry up, and even today it is found here and there, especially in the Catholic and Quaker traditions. It may be that the neo-mystic movement, now centered in California, is rediscovering a vital resource of Christianity, which Christianity will eventually absorb to its own enrichment.

It seems unlikely that pure, unadulterated mysticism could ever outdistance all rivals. Buddhism began as practically that, but quickly acquired a priesthood, ritual, and all the trappings. It became almost as sharp-edged as

Christianity. The difference is that Christianity was apparently sharp-edged from the beginning.

Perhaps everyone has the latent potentialities for undertaking the mystic's quest but not everyone can be persuaded. A religion must try to bring out the spiritual possibilities in each person, but it must also recognize differences in temperament. Christianity, like all widespread religions, has tacitly done this. It offers the way of sainthood to those willing to pay the price, and the path of moral commandments, faith, prayer, sacraments, and church attendance to the more humdrum. Any religion which demanded 100 per cent sainthood or mysticism would drive many of its followers to despair, apathy, or astrologers.

However, I am weary of pragmatic considerations. The revival of Christianity will depend on whether it is true. If it *is* true, then each of us is created by God with an innate desire to know and serve the truth. Try as we will, nothing less than the truth will satisfy our hunger. We may search desperately for substitutes: there are none. Christianity also teaches that God Himself is always ready to aid the search for truth; that if we are willing to face the truth, God will give it to us.

The question, then, comes back to one of fact. If Christianity is true, Christianity will revive, because men are created to seek truth. Since, as I have explained, this is not a book of apologetics, I shall not try to prove the truth of Christianity. I shall leave the matter at this point, and assume—for purposes of discussion—that Christianity is true and that therefore the world will turn to it.

PART TWO

The Shape of Things to Come

4

The Rediscovery of Reason, Free Will, and Hope

Christianity is a religion which strains the limits of credulity and at the same time confirms the faith of the common man in common sense.

The first aspect, which is a serious stumbling block to many, entails violent contrasts and paradoxes. The doctrine of the Trinity is an excellent instance. We are told that God is one but that He is also three. Thomas Jefferson stumbled at its arithmetic, and many others have stumbled with him. The Trinity is what theologians call a "supernatural mystery." Socrates and Plato never surmised it, for the reason that it could not be evolved by sheer thought. It had to be revealed. Only after Christ's followers had come to recognize His divinity could they know that God is not monolithic—that within the unity of one God there are at least two distinctions or "Persons." And only after the experience of Pentecost, when new understanding and wild courage filled them, could they understand the third Person, the Holy Ghost. The doctrine of the Trinity, therefore, rests not on reason but on the experience of the Christian community—and, ultimately, on the Revelation of God.

It is not necessary to delve into so recondite a dogma as the Trinity to find a basic teaching of Christianity which

61

taxes credulity. The Incarnation by itself suffices. Not that it seems unreasonable to assume that God could become man if He chose to—the marvel is that He chose. We humans know what love is, but our love has its limits. We certainly would not die for a species below our own. The great obstacle to believing in the Incarnation is not intellectual but moral.

These two examples are sufficient to dispel any idea that Christianity is a series of "obvious" religious truths. Christianity is not religion but *a* religion, and its edges are sharp. But equally important is the other aspect of Christianity—the down-to-earth, common-sense side. No sooner does the Christian's head begin floating in the clouds of metaphysics than his feet are rudely forced back to the solid earth.

Christianity says that the universe was created, and that it was created neither by a lunatic nor a devil. It was created by a Being who is absolute perfection—perfect power, perfect intellect, perfect moral nature. Such a universe should be expected to make sense; it should be more like a symphony than a surrealist painting. Christianity also teaches that we can understand large parts of this universe. We can do this because we are "created in the image" of its Creator. It is easy to slide glibly over this phrase without realizing its vast and heartening significance. Obviously it does not mean that our bodies look like God; God is a Being "without body, parts, or passions." It must mean that we share—in a lesser and imperfect degree, of course—the attributes of God. We have a moral nature with which to perceive the unchanging moral order of the universe, no matter how often we go counter to what we perceive; we have the capacity to love and respond to love; we have minds that can think.

In the long run, science and any other kind of objective

knowledge are dependent on the belief that man is created in the image of God. If man just happens to be, then his thoughts just happen to be, and the thoughts of Einstein and those of the village idiot are equally valid. The Christianity of the future, by underlining the fact of reason, should give added stimulus to the development of science. But the rediscovery of reason will not be the private treasure of the scientists. To everyone the possession of thinking minds will come as a liberation. Reason exists; independently of the urge to make money, childhood conditioning, biology and Freud, reason exists.

This is not to say that man is a thinking machine and nothing else. Such an idea is not a Christian doctrine but the heresy of some rationalists. Man is both more and less than a thinking machine. His power to think is tainted by self-centeredness, as anyone can see when the conversation turns to politics and economics. It is also muddied by the inherent limitations of creaturehood. Though made by God, we are not God. We are entangled in the physical universe; our bodies are a part of it. It is a universe we did not design, and we cannot hope to understand every last atom of it, though we shall someday understand much more than we do today. We are held accountable to moral laws we did not legislate, and our intuitive perception of them has to be supplemented and reinforced by Revelation. In short, God gave us all the intellectual rope we need, but the monomaniacal daydreams of Dr. Faustus remain forever illusory.

The second rediscovery will be free will. It is so closely associated with reason that little needs to be added to what I have just said, but perhaps a brief postscript is in order.

The main Christian tradition dramatizes free will as no other faith does. Christ died for the salvation of all mankind; "in principle," we are all saved. But there is a crucial difference between "in principle" and "in deed." God does not force salvation down any man's throat. Each individual must willingly accept what is willingly offered. He cannot remain on the fence. The idea of drastic alternatives runs through Christianity: "He that is not with me, is against me"; "And if thy right eye offend thee, pluck it out, and cast it from thee: for it is profitable for thee that one of thy members should perish, and not that thy whole body should be cast into hell"; "No man can serve two masters"; "He that findeth his life, shall lose it: and he that loseth his life for my sake, shall find it."

The rediscovery of free will is destined to wreak havoc on alibis. We shall no longer be able to blame everything on complexes and childhood misfortunes. Free will is complicated by irrational factors, but it still exists. The man who was taught as a child to hate Negroes is not thereby excused if he placidly continues to hate them after he knows better. He can choose to continue hating, or choose to make the attempt to love.

A belief in free will and reason will get the men of good will out of their squirrel cage of determinism. The man who desires "one world" will no longer pessimistically assume that the cards are hopelessly stacked against him by centuries of mass conditioning in tribal loyalties. He will simply recognize the difficulties for what they are and go ahead to combat them. Knowing that he has free will to believe in a world federation, he gives everyone else the benefit of the doubt by assuming that they are potentially as free as he is. The man fighting for reforms on the home front will not fatalistically rule out the possibility of co-operation from the most unlikely sources: the Boston Brahman may surprise him by turning crusader for industrial democracy.

This leads to the rediscovery of hope—a state of mind gravely lacking at the core of the modern consciousness, no matter how cheerful the official statements to the press. Christianity stimulates hope in several additional ways. The most obvious is the doctrine of Immortality. What happens on the earth is not the whole story. The moral nature of the universe is vindicated in the long run, in each individual life; no loose ends of injustice are left when the final accounting is made.

Another strong source of encouragement is the doctrine of original sin. It is curious that this dogma arouses such violent antagonism among modern thinkers; next to the belief in hell it is the most unpopular clause of Christian theology. But original sin, whatever the historical events back of it, simply means that everyone without exception has a tendency toward evil. There are no boundary lines. Rich and poor, ignorant and educated, Christian and non-Christian, all share at least one heritage in common. The truth of the doctrine is so self-evident that one need not turn Christian in order to accept it. Any history text consists four-fifths of chapters describing the social consequences of original sin. The newspaper headlines are full of it. Any playground, with children ganging up on one unfortunate and tormenting him out of sheer perverseness, is as good as an old-fashioned Calvinistic sermon. There is a certain nobility about our common affliction: it does not seek material gains or even happiness. It brings bitterness and misery to the possessor as well as to the victim.

But I have said that original sin is a cause for hope. I am not attempting a subtle paradox. I merely mean that the doctrine eliminates one of the main sources of despair. The reformer and the do-gooder are always in a vulnerable position. Their plans never turn out quite as planned. Without belief in original sin, it is easy to develop a feeling that fate or the "breaks" are against you—or a still blacker belief that human nature, instead of being completely good, is completely bad. Many reformers have ended their lives as soured old men because they hoped for too much when they began.

Original sin makes you reckon from the beginning with the certainty that something will go amiss. If things turn out approximately as planned, you are so pleased that you do not fret too much at the minor dislocations and failures. Nothing contributes more to a mellow, cheerful view of the world than a steadfast belief in original sin. It combats tenseness and overanxiety, with the result that progress toward a better society becomes more likely. And in personal relationships the doctrine is one of the main inspirations toward a charitable viewpoint in dealing with other people. It is perhaps disconcerting to think of the world as one huge hospital, and all of us patients in it, but close observers have often noticed that people suffering from the same affliction are drawn together and sustain one another by helpfulness and understanding.

It would be overly dour to leave the matter at this point. The greatest source of hope is what I mentioned earlier: the Christian, unlike the humanist, is not completely on his own. Strength and guidance are his for the asking. When he goes to church with his neighbors; when he receives the sacraments or prays in his room; when he loves God and loves his neighbors or consciously refuses to conform to the shallow goals of secularism—at all these times he is letting down the barriers between himself and God, and once the barriers are lowered he receives the help that makes the decisive difference in his life.

First the Individual

In the earlier part of this book I was obliged to say many glum things about the present period of history. To round out the picture, praise should be given where praise is due. Our age is pre-eminent in one thing: sensitivity to social, political, and economic problems. The human conscience, in some periods scarcely reaching beyond the neighbor next door, has been socially and geographically enlarged. The residents of New York City worry about the share-croppers in Georgia. An earthquake in Japan or a famine in India arouses sympathy in every literate country, and the relief ships come from all directions.

This widening of the sense of responsibility is the real moral accomplishment of the modern period. It can be partly explained by the development of communications and transport systems, but, whatever the reasons, the accomplishment is a genuine one. If it is preserved and carried further, it will live on as a permanent moral gain after many things that are generally admired—technology, applied science, methods of education, mass entertainment—are judged by the future with qualified "Yes's" and "No's." Whether it will survive is touch and go. Nazism, which came closer to total victory than we care to remember, was a disciplined effort to jail the conscience inside the stone walls of nation and race; other ideologies advocate other stone walls.

But assuming that the builders of walls are frustrated, the extension of conscience is still hamstrung by unbelievable naïveté in the methods employed to improve specific conditions. Superplanning is hailed as the universal panacea. Here and there the plans have been put into effect, with the able backing of administrators, technicians, and policemen. The results are not encouraging. The old problems simply change their names. The planners and the planned remain stubbornly human, and are quick to take personal advantage of possibilities inside the new framework.

Russia is the best example both because of the genuine idealism that inspired her revolution and the thoroughness of her planning. Thirty years after the revolution to establish a classless state, Stalin = the Czar; the Politburo = the inner circle of court advisers; the Communist party = the aristocracy; and the MVD = the Cheka. The two indisputable gains have been increased technological and military efficiency and an unequaled system of indoctrination to convince the masses that they like what they are powerless to alter.

It is unjust to single Russia out for unique condemnation. To a lesser degree similiar results can be seen everywhere. Russia is simply the most dramatic case study of the futility of trying to eradicate social ills by planning and nothing but planning.

The facts of human nature are the monkey wrenches. Mankind possesses cunning. In any social system it will find an outlet. One can intrigue and look out for Number One on a collective farm as well as in a Chevrolet factory. The top planners are likely to be especially intelligent— and therefore well equipped to advance their private interests (which, by an easy quirk of the mind, they invariably identify with the public welfare).

It must be confessed that during the last few decades a number of church leaders have fallen into the trap of believing that all human problems can be solved by reform campaigns and social planning. The frequent criticism that the churches meddle in politics is no valid complaint, but there is cause for discontent when the churches put their entire reliance on politics and pressure campaigns. With some all-out adherents of the "social gospel" that has happened, and their viewpoint and activities have become indistinguishable from those of the secular reformer. If planning and politics are the complete answer, then the whole campaign for a better world might as well rest on nonreligious foundations.

Fortunately, an increasing Christian sophistication is bringing the churches back to the psychological insight of traditional Christianity. Church people are learning, or relearning, that there is no short cut, no road to social improvement that by-passes the individual. Plans are necessary, but the best plans will fail unless the individuals in society become radically different from what they are in their unredeemed state. Everything that Christ taught and all the implications of Christian theology point unambiguously to this conclusion.

Plans deal with that abstraction "society." Religion dares strike at what is wrong with the individual. Christianity pictures the individual as a vast battlefield within. The struggle is a complex one. The two main camps are good and evil. Evil is not merely the result of bad environment or bad economics; it is something inherent in man's present nature, and would still remain to plague him in the most benign social order conceivable. Within the camp of evil, constant brawls break out. One evil impulse conflicts with another; for example, lust and drunkenness get in each other's way, and both clash with mercenary ambition.

The only time the forces of evil will consent to sincere co-operation is in their permanent war against the forces of good. In this conflict the varied forms of evil prove advantageous; an army equipped with heavy artillery, tanks, and planes can conduct a more versatile campaign than one consisting entirely of infantry.

If we were not familiar almost from birth with this inner war, it would strike us as extremely odd. The animals can apparently boast nothing analogous; the nature of a mouse or a lion is all of one piece. Man is the only house divided. The Christian explanation is telescoped in the story of Adam and Eve. It is a tale of a splendid beginning and a ruinous downfall. Man, as designed by God, did not carry a battlefield inside him. As long as he made God the center of his life he was in joyous harmony with himself, God, and his neighbors. The schism in human nature began when man ejected God from the central position and set himself up on a makeshift throne. Instantly, dozens of clamorous demands arose. The new center was inadequate to maintain harmony. Each facet of the personality warred with every other, and each individual man was in competition with his fellows.

Christianity is a vast process initiated by God Himself to undo what Adam and Eve accomplished for us. The result cannot be brought about by decrees nailed to the courthouse door. Just as man used his free will to disobey God and "fall," so each of us has free will to accept—or reject— the work of restoration that God is willing to begin inside us.

The temperament of the individual does not matter. He does not have to be a mystic; he does not have to be emotional; he does not have to be highly educated. Christianity

is a religion that can transform everyone, from Thomas
Aquinas to the most illiterate peasant; Aquinas could not
exhaust its subtleties, and the peasant can understand
enough of it to become, not figuratively but literally, a
new creature.

The core of Christianity is the conviction that Christ is
both God and man. In Christ one sees the supreme glory of
God—His outgoing, sacrificial love—translated into human
terms, into concreteness, so that our minds, largely chained
to the human and material, can grasp what it means. This
love is without limits; it led to the Crucifixion, where the
impossible weight of human sin was borne by God Himself. At the same time, Christ is completely human. One
might say that He is the only complete human being of
whom we have any knowledge, for every deed and word of
His show humanity as it was originally meant to be, and as
God intends it yet to be.

The unique glory of Christ the man did not come from
a negative struggle against warring forces within Him. It
came from an unquestioning surrender to God. And the
way open to the Christian is the same. By his knowledge of
Christ, he knows what God is like. Only by an act of the
will, only by a surrender of his whole being to God, can he
make a start toward becoming what, on a smaller scale, he
is meant to be—an *alter Christus.*

This does not mean that the individual disappears in
God like a raindrop in the ocean. Christianity differs from
some varieties of mysticism by insisting that personality is
eternal. To put it figuratively, the man from Maine who
arrives in heaven will still speak with a down-East twang,
and the North Carolina tobacco farmer will delight the
angels with his drolleries. Surrender to God is not a merger
but a transformation.

The surrender, however many years it may take, is

essential. Everything else depends on it. Most Christians find the process a lifelong one, with much left to be finished after death. It is a day-by-day battle inside the self. One day the moral sense, reinforced by the Grace of God, gains ground; the next day, a counterattack, spearheaded by pride, greed, or lust, and aided by treachery within the will, recovers the lost terrain and far more. The field of battle is ordinarily more reminiscent of the trenches and slow advances of World War I than of the swift mechanized battles of the recent war, though occasionally advances of blitzkrieg rapidity are made by one side or the other and the battle map is revolutionized overnight.

It may be sensibly asked what difference God makes, if the individual must still fight constant battles inside himself. The answer is that God makes all the difference the individual is willing to let Him make. As long as a man's faith remains firm and his *will* is directed toward God, he can recover from temporary setbacks and then advance to new victories. He may have his Dunkirks and Bataans, but never a Waterloo.

These military comparisons are the best one can do, but they have an unpleasant ring. The final result is anything but suggestive of the tumult of battle; it is closer to the uncommunicable music that is heard once or twice in a life-time. The keywords of Christian psychology are not battle and anxiety but peace and love and joy.

The thing has an unmistakable taste. It can be sampled in the writings of the medieval mystics, and the same taste is found in such modern works as *A Testament of Devotion,* by the late Thomas R. Kelly. The taste can be sensed from reading, but, of course, the experience that lies back of it cannot be fully grasped except by the person who to some extent has known it in his own life. There is an existential quality about Christianity; the only person who can understand Christianity with any depth is the person who is already a Christian—hence the futility of most religious arguments.

All I have said about the peace and joy that Christians, when far enough advanced, find in their faith may suggest that the rewards are purely personal. The individual finds a new harmony inside himself, but what good is that to society? Is the old taunt that religion is antisocial and selfishly individualistic justified?

The questions deserve to be answered in the practical language in which they are asked. First of all, the individual whose life is centered in God is no longer a prey to constant fear and anxiety. He can act without constantly peering over his shoulder to see what unnamed demons are lurking behind him. Death itself becomes an incident in a story which begins in time but will continue outside time. With many psychological distractions eliminated or lessened, it becomes possible to act with more simplicity, directness, and efficiency. In the second place, the individual becomes more and more capable of loving as God loves—without asking for anything in return. This is considerably different from ordinary human love, which usually involves an implication of "I'll give this if you give that." The closest natural analogy is parental love, but even the love of a parent for his child is always mixed with egoism. As the higher kind of love grows, personal hate recedes and vanishes; the Christian who is far advanced can and should hate the sin, but never the sinner. In the third place, the new kind of love is not competitive. Rather, it works to overcome the impulse to exploit other people. Real co-operation at last becomes possible. Finally, the Christian has the most convincing grounds for courage and hope. He does not put his main trust in social schemes or in human nature, but in God the Creator and Friend of all men. He knows that though one specific panacea may fail, and then another, mankind is not lost. For the redemptive process initiated by Christ is at work, and there is a way, slow and painful though it may be, for the individual—and through him, society—to become remade.

The connection between total surrender to God and social behavior was stated with admirable brevity by Christ Himself. One of the Pharisees asked Him, "Which is the great commandment in the law?" Christ replied, "Thou shalt love the Lord thy God with all thy heart, and with all thy soul, and with all thy mind. This is the first and great commandment. And the second is like unto it, Thou shalt love thy neighbor as thyself. On these two commandments hang all the law and the prophets."

Here, then, is the great divide between the Christian and the secular idealist. The latter says that you should start by loving your neighbor. The Christian insists that the attempt is a psychological impossibility; the individual is in such turmoil inside that he will never get very far with loving his neighbor unless he first loves God—love for his neighbor will then spring up as an overwhelming by-product.

The inevitable words of qualification are needed at this point. I have been speaking of the consequences of Christianity when the individual goes very far toward complete love of God. Obviously, many halt midway. And always there is the danger that egoism will cloak itself in piety and make of religion a peculiarly detestable mask for selfishness. Sin can use religion as it uses everything else. But at any rate, a little genuine religious progress on the part of a large number of people would add up to very much. If this were supplemented and strengthened by a fair number of saints, the impact on society would take on the proportions of a revolution.

Saints have always been rare, though in some ages not as rare as during our present materialistic period. When they have appeared in history they have changed it. St. Francis, whose friars were for a long time the only social workers in the slums of medieval Europe; Elizabeth Fry, venturing into filthy prisons to bring human compassion to the prisoners; the English evangelicals in their war against the slave trade; Father Damien, living among the lepers of Hawaii and cheerfully accepting leprosy as his reward; Albert Schweitzer, now in his seventies, working a twelve-hour day to provide medical care for the natives of French Equatorial Africa—all are men and women who loved God so completely that they loved their neighbors, near and far, as themselves.

Christianity does not deny that other religions have their saints; God will meet whoever sincerely seeks Him. Gandhi was such a saint, and there are others. But it can be maintained—on the purely pragmatic level—that Christianity is the religion most likely to transform the man who is not a religious genius. It is spiritually democratic. Christ is God translated into humanity. Anyone who knows of Christ knows what God is and knows also what man can be. It is much easier to serve a Man-God than an Unconditioned Absolute or Prime Mover.

Christianity and social planning are not enemies. In any conceivable society, plans will still be needed. Not every individual will ask for God's transforming power, nor respond completely to it—in any earth that we can even dream of, original sin will remain and there must be some sort of social structure to protect the rights of as many as possible. There must be organized efforts to combat evil wherever it appears, to eradicate misery wherever found. The Christian will feel this obligation more keenly than other men, for he has caught a glimpse of God's love—and knows that his burden and privilege is "to be his brother's keeper."

But he will never fall into the illusion of believing that evil men can plan and create a good society. The greater the number of men transformed wholly or partially into sons of God, the better the prospects that social planning will not prove a detour to new injustices and tyrannies.

๛ 6 ๛

Society *Sub Specie Aeternitatis*

If anyone reads the New Testament for detailed outlines
of the ideal society he will be disappointed. The attempt
has been made and elaborate programs drawn up, but only
by reading Christ's mind instead of His recorded words.
Almost willfully, it seems, Christ talked of man and God
and of man and his neighbor, but beyond a few general
statements about the duties a citizen owes to his government, He said little that can be put into a political platform.

Such is the first and disappointing impression. A second
or third reading of the New Testament, supplemented by
a study of the Old Testament and consideration of basic
Christian theology, suddenly reveals that while Christianity
does not answer the countless specific questions that arise
in a complex society, it does provide a number of very
definite principles by which to test any social system. Some
of these principles may be listed:

1. As we saw in the last chapter, love—unselfish, un-
demanding love—is the basis of Christian living. It begins
with love for God and expands (ideally) into love for every
man. In the golden rule, the principle of love is given an
activist slant: "All things whatsoever ye would that men
should do to you, do ye even so to them." It is not enough
to refrain from elbowing other people out of the way. We

77

are commanded to go out of our own way to help them—
without asking anything in return.

2. The things we are told to do for our neighbors are
frequently prosaic. Christ speaks of feeding the hungry,
giving drinks of water to the thirsty, clothing the naked, and
providing medical care for the injured.

3. The social nature of Christianity is still further high-
lighted by Christ's constant teachings about the Kingdom
of God. For our present purposes it does not greatly matter
whether He believed it would come into being by a supernatural intervention into history or whether it would be
built up gradually. In any case, it would involve a drastic
alteration of society, with love and unselfish co-operation
replacing the profit motive. It seems clear that Christ regarded the Kingdom as already existing in some fashion
among His followers. "The kingdom of God is within you,"
he said, or, as some translators render it, "The kingdom of
God is in the midst of you."

4. The concept of the Church which prevailed in New
Testament days and is still held by the great majority of
Christians was an organic one. The Church is not a loose
organization of like-minded people bound together by pep
talks, every-member canvasses, and bingo parties. It is a
"body," consisting of all Christians, living or dead. The
"head" of the body is Christ. Misfortune cannot befall one
"member" of the body without every other member being
affected, any more than the arm can remain in splendid iso-
lation while the leg rots with gangrene.

5. Christianity is not as "spiritual" as some would wish
it to be. Genesis bluntly states that God created the universe
and considered it good. This sets Judaism and Christianity
in irreconcilable opposition to a great swarm of Oriental
religions and modern cults which regard the material world

as an invention of the devil or at best a meaningless, neutral thing. It is true that man has succeeded in misusing the good thing that God created—dust bowls and the atomic bomb are man's achievement, not God's. But the material universe remains basically glorious and good; so good that each of us will have some sort of physical body given to us when we rise from death.

6. The central Christian doctrine of the Incarnation is in itself sufficient answer to any attempt to overspiritualize Christianity. The Incarnation means that the world of sticks, stones, atoms, and bodies is so good and rich in possibilities that God was willing and able to become part of it.

7. Finally, a strong note of sacramentalism runs through Christianity. It comes out most vividly in the Lord's Supper. The different churches vary in their interpretation of it, ranging from the Roman Catholic insistence that the bread and wine are changed into the "substance" of the body and blood of Christ, to the liberal Protestant belief that the service is only symbolic. But throughout Christian history most Christians have been convinced that in one mode or another Christ is literally present. It is worth noting that Christ did not specify expensive imported cakes and an esoteric kind of wine for the one religious service that He established. It was plain bread and plain wine—the household food and drink of the time. He deliberately chose the most commonplace things, as though to emphasize that God is present in the workshop, on the farm, and in the market place.

These seven points may seem a highly theoretical prologue to a discussion of politics and economics. Actually they are not. Several simple conclusions emerge: (1) The material world, though often misused, is basically good. (2) We are bodies as well as spirits; we need not be ashamed of wanting to eat, live in houses, and be clothed. (3) We are all in the same boat together; every man is his brother's keeper.

The conclusions I have just listed are sufficient to put an end to the hideous nonsense preached around the turn of the century by many eminent sociologists who misunderstood and perverted the discoveries of Darwin. I mean the theory that the unfortunate should be allowed to starve in the ditch by the roadside, for such is the survival of the fittest. Of all social theories that have ever been advanced, this was the most monstrous. Medieval feudalism, modern communism, even Nazism (for the Nazis did at least look after their Nazi brothers) were more compatible with Christianity than this apotheosis of rugged individualism. Christian society is not a jungle but an organism. If the village half-wit dies of malnutrition, the whole social body is the poorer.

How the hungry shall be fed and the shelterless housed brings up the general question of economic systems. Here Christianity implies a frankly pragmatic position. The system is best which gets the job done and at the same time avoids concentrating tyrannical power in the hands of a few. Original sin is the constant factor at all times. It produces social inequalities and injustices; then, when the power of society is invoked to provide remedies, it quietly goes to work on a higher level to create new injustices. This is seen most clearly in the case of revolutions. The leaders of the revolution make a clean sweep of ancient abuses, then proceed to entrench themselves in power and reap the rewards of power. The tightrope walk that any society, bent upon reform, must undertake is to cure one set of injustices without giving so much power into the hands of an army of administrators and leaders that the last condition is worse than the first.

If it were not for original sin, a communistic economy would probably be logical for a Christian society, and it would be reasonable enough to choose one intelligent man and give him general control over the whole system, for the sake of efficiency. But—since original sin *does* exist as the most important of all sociological facts—any system that bestows great power on one man or a handful of men is certain to lead to tyrannical abuses. It does not matter whether the system is ideally the best one or not—the concentration of power will corrupt it.

But if communism is bad because it leads to tyranny, old-fashioned capitalism is bad for the same reason. The conservative of the old school, if at all idealistic, believed that some mysterious law of nature would guarantee progress and an eventual heaven on earth once business was given its head. This faith was psychologically akin to the Communist belief that history moves inevitably toward the millennium of the classless state. Nothing worked out as the conservative planned. Business was unwilling to abide by the rules of the game. Instead of plunging into a genuine junglelike struggle, the various firms began to form combines, trusts, and cartels for the express purpose of making the jungle inhabitable for themselves, if not for the rivals that insisted on real rugged individualism. Wages, instead of being determined by supply and demand, were fixed by the heads of vast monopolies; prices were determined in smoke-filled rooms.

The system broke down because the players didn't really believe in the rules of the game. They were ruggedly individualistic if anyone suggested a bit of regulation in the interest of the public, but the rest of their time they were busy devising subterfuges to cheat the immutable natural laws of economics. Labor and the general public finally woke up to the anomaly of the situation. Labor unions, regulatory legislation, and the bloodless revolution of the New Deal were a tacit recognition that rugged individualism was never much more than a theoretical concept. The tendency throughout the world has been toward the same realism; some countries, while not Communist, have gone much further in the direction of social control than has prosperous America.

Apart from the invaluable doctrine of original sin, what insights does Christianity have to contribute? It is clear that to regard capitalism or socialism or communism as the necessary handmaiden of Christianity is to fall into the heresy that C. S. Lewis' "Screwtape" calls "Christianity and————." No one economic system has a right to attach itself to the skirts of the Church and to ask for a free ride. Feudalism tried to do this during the Middle Ages; then capitalism; some varieties of socialism have also made the attempt; here and there Communist-minded theorists voice their demand. All are asking what Christianity cannot grant without becoming a mere appendage.

At the same time, Christianity has a great deal to say about economics. Anything that tends to level up gross differences in income is desirable because it conforms to justice (the social expression of Christian love) so long as the system proposed does not establish a tyranny worse than the economic abuses which it cures. The graduated income tax is Christian, the sales tax on food and clothing less certainly so. The right of private property, sometimes regarded as an absolute, is nothing of the sort; the Christian property owner is a "steward" for what God has created, and if he is a poor steward he has no claim to the support of the Church when society calls him in for an accounting. For example, no landowner has an absolute right to cut all the trees on his property if the resulting deforestation will fill the near-by river with silt.

The most desirable economy will vary from country to country, depending on its history, social institutions, and technological development. For a country like America, the various considerations would seem to point toward a mixed, inconsistent economy, such as the Scandinavian countries have been evolving for some years. Neither the capitalist nor the Communist will like it. A process of trial and error may reveal that natural monopolies are best owned by the government, or at least subjected to strict regulation, whereas medium and small businesses and farming can be left in private hands. To make the economy still more pluralistic (thus guarding against dangerous concentrations of power), an extensive development of consumers' co-operatives would be very wholesome, and peculiarly in keeping with the neighborly spirit of Christianity. Labor unions, by providing another source of power, are an additional safeguard against tyrannical business or tyrannical government. The whole picture is not an idyllic one; it is not the Kingdom of God. But if society, in a fallen world, can keep enough balance to walk the tightrope, it has adequate cause for rejoicing.

Such an economy would still include large patches of jungle. The churches can do a great deal to train the conscience of its members so that they will behave a bit less like ape men. They must teach manufacturer, union member, farmer, and consumer alike that morality concerns not only man-to-man relations, but also dealings between capital and labor, farmer and city dweller, the business firm and its rivals. To do this would be to return to the role of the medieval Church, and to begin drawing the scattered provinces of society back into a co-operative federation. A promising start has already been made by several recent popes in their encyclicals, and by such pronouncements as those of the Anglicans at the Malvern Conference in 1941. It will be up to the churches to teach that morality is indivisible, that there is no field of activity which is morally neutral, that underhanded business methods are as much a violation of Christian morality as running off with a rival's wife. The churches, of course, cannot talk society into perfect unselfishness, but they can do a great deal to bestow the precious gift of an uneasy conscience.

This discussion of the future Christian society—particularly its economy—has so far been filled with the vague generalities that I condemned in my Foreword. There is a reason for this, and here I must clearly speak in the first person and not presume to interpret the general viewpoint of Christians.

All the implications of Christianity suggest strongly to me that the most deep-seated economic malady of the Western world (and here I include Russia) is one that has little to do with the relative merits of capitalism and socialism and communism, and is not likely to be remedied by any of the proposed cures. The malady is the twin worship of gadgets and bigness.

By gadgets I mean an infinite number of articles, mostly invented in recent years and mass-produced in large factories—automobiles, electric toasters, radios, fancy attachments to lawn hoses, mix-masters, electric razors, and the like. These devices and hundreds like them are not inventions of Satan. He merely turns them to his purposes, by encouraging the unsophisticated to worship them as ends in themselves.

The writers of advertisements are lavishly paid to make us forget the distinction between the gadgets we need and those we think we need. In city life, an electric refrigerator may be essential; in the country the old-fashioned spring-house will keep milk cool. An automobile is a necessity to a physician, a questionable luxury for most urbanites. Many gadgets are purchased, not because they are needed, but because the neighbors possess them.

Another aspect of the gadget, which the Christian must consider seriously, is that many of them are so nearly use-less that a thoughful Christian would hesitate to spend eight hours a day making them. Man is meant to share in God's creativeness. One can imagine God turning baker but not juke-box maker. Many men and women spend the best part of their energy for forty years or more making things so trivial or downright harmful that an intelligent child would go on strike in a week's time. And there is no way of making a psychological break between what one does from nine to five, and what is done after the day's work is over. If the day's work is trivial, the triviality will color the evening. It is true that the gadget-maker is paid for his work, and uses his pay to provide food for the hungry mouths at home. But a Christian society should not compel its members to choose between empty vocations and empty stomachs.

Another serious charge against the gadget is that it is typically made in large factories. Here we come to the ques-tion of bigness. In a large plant, card files take the place of personal contact between employer and employee. The worker knows his straw boss; but the owner of the factory is merely the greedy old exploiter whose picture appears in the society column. The owner, no matter what he might desire, cannot possibly get to know his men personally; they remain vague abstractions in his mind, and at best he treats them as humanely as the horses in his stables. The assembly-line system of production, which is constantly being adapted to new items of manufacture, is perhaps the most dehumanizing factor of all. The worker becomes an automaton, endlessly repeating the same motions, and concerned only with one tiny detail of the finished article. He is deprived of his natural reward—a feeling of creative accomplishment. The testimony of men who have worked in modern factories is almost unanimous: that the monotony of the labor can be endured only after something of spontaneous joy is killed in the individual; a fully alive man cannot take it.

To make matters still less favorable for the Christian life (or even a decent pagan life), the gadget factory is usually located in or near large cities. The big city has already reached the state of overdevelopment attained by prehistoric monsters when their armor grew so heavy that they starved for lack of mobility. A strike of truck drivers can plunge the city into famine. Traffic jams at certain times of day make travel almost impossible. Decent housing for the masses is a geographical impossibility.

The breakdown of any sense of community reaches its climax in the city. One can see this in the curiously impersonal way that passers-by glance at one another. The stranger senses it most of all, for he is more completely alone in a city of six million than in a town of six thousand.

I do not say that a Christian life is impossible in the cities. God can perform miracles when man is willing. I do believe that the cards are stacked against the individual, and that fewer people can make the grade in the city than in small towns and the country. For the average man to have a fighting chance of living a Christian life he needs at least two things: (1) some worthy way to exercise his creative instinct; and (2) genuine human relationships outside the four walls of his house or apartment. The gadget-maker, working in a huge factory and living in a monstrous city, seldom has either.

There is nothing Rousseauistic about this. Rousseau's illusion was to believe that men are naturally good, which they are not. The small town is no sylvan paradise; human nature can be as nasty and petty there as in New York. But the small town and farm do have many advantages. One is that the sins one commits have visible moral consequences. The writer of a syndicated gossip column may never see the people whose reputation he ruins; the village gossip must face the wrath or tears of her victim, and may thereby be moved to repentance or at least caution. In the same way, there is more possibility of a Christian relationship between employer and employee in small businesses. The owner and workers can know one another, argue, lose their tempers face-to-face, and sometimes love one another.

If decentralization took place, it is likely that fewer gadgets would be produced and that more creative energy would be spent on genuinely useful things, like food, furniture, housing, etc.—most of which do not require vast establishments for their production. Certain gadgets, which serve a genuine purpose and require large factories to produce, would still have to be manufactured in the huge plants, but the number of such items might turn out to be smaller than everyone assumes if once the technicians set to work to find ways of making them in smaller shops. In any event, there is no need for most of the large plants to cluster around a few dozen cities.

What I am imagining here is the only really radical economic revolution possible. Communism merely substitutes the state for the cartel director. Decentralization would create a large number of small and relatively harmless entrepreneurs, and would encourage one-man and family businesses. To some extent this would be turning the hands on the clock back. That is no valid criticism unless one believes in inevitable progress, which I do not. However, decentralization would not be a mere reversion to the economy of the seventeenth century. Developments like the TVA can provide electrical power for small shops and farms, eliminating much brutalizing drudgery; atomic energy, if used for peaceful purposes, holds similar promise; applied science and technology, if directed toward small-scale operations, can keep production costs from rising to the luxury-goods level.

I think faint but significant indications can be detected of a trend toward decentralization. More and more city people are finding that they cannot bring up their children as civilized beings unless they flee to the suburbs, and the suburbs are getting constantly farther away from the city. The present situation is an uneasy compromise. The father rises early, spends forty-five minutes on the interurban riding to work, works, catches the interurban at five fifteen, and returns to the quiet suburban home where his wife and the children have meanwhile been living human lives. The next stage will come when the fathers in the suburb demand to know why their work cannot be in walking distance of their homes. Once such talk begins, the really radical revolution is under way. And when it starts, I suspect it will pick up powerful support from an awakened Christianity.

So far I have said very little about political systems, except where they are entangled with economic problems. It cannot be proved that one particular system is *necessarily* required by Christianity. It is possible, however, to rule out some systems because they make it impossible for the

average person to live a Christian life. For example, any
kind of totalitarianism—or democracy for that matter—
which enforces the idolatrous worship of race, state, etc.,
or commands its citizens to do abominable things like mur-
dering innocent people by some variety of euthanasia. But
apart from clear-cut cases like Nazi Germany, there is no
reason in theory why a Christian society should not be a
monarchy or aristocracy, if the king or nobles were benevolent. The only catch is that they seldom are. Like dictators,
they are bloated with pride and ambition. And the people
have no effective control over them. Politicians in democratic countries are also lacking in perfection, but the
people have ways of holding them in check. The rascals
can always be thrown out. Therefore—more for pragmatic
than theoretical reasons—democracy seems the best possibility, at least for countries with sufficient maturity to
manage it.

The best way of stating the relationship between democracy and Christianity is to say that Christianity does not
require democracy but that democracy seems to require
Christianity. If, for common-sense reasons, democracy
appears the system most likely to avoid tyranny and to
develop the maximum of social justice, Christianity is the
psychological and spiritual foundation on which it can rest
most securely. Except for the brief-lived Athenian experiment in democracy (actually an oligarchy, since most of
the population was not permitted to vote), every democracy that has been reasonably successful over a period of
years has been in countries that are largely Christian now
or whose attitudes have been saturated with Christian
assumptions in the past.

Discussing this relationship in *The Atlantic Monthly* of

December, 1947, Barbara Ward[1] listed several definite
attitudes that are essential to the success of democracy and
pointed out their Christian genesis. (This is not to deny
that other religions might produce these attitudes; we can
deal only with what has already happened.) Miss Ward's
analysis is more detailed and penetrating than any I could
attempt, and any person concerned about the future of
democracy would be well advised to read it carefully. One
of the points she makes is that Christianity involves belief
in a moral order which has an absolute validity; it cannot
be annulled or modified to suit the convenience of men or
their society. When the drafters of the Declaration of Independence spoke of "unalienable rights," they were consciously or unconsciously relying upon this assumption. It
is still the strongest barrier in democratic countries against
any despotic leanings on the part of the elected government, or even on the part of a majority of the population. In
other words, the majority is not absolutely free to do anything it wants to in regard to the minority.

Miss Ward also enumerates the Christian doctrine of the
Fatherhood of God, from which springs the belief that
human personality is of infinite value and all human souls
are essentially equal. This assumption, so clearly necessary
for democracy, rests on an act of faith, for the inequality
of human intelligence and character is undeniable.

A third contribution of Christianity is the idea of sin,
which leads to a realization of human fallibility and a willingness to seek working compromises rather than carry out
wholesale liquidations of those who oppose the policies
of the leaders or the majority.

Finally, Christianity inculcates the virtue of pity, and with

[1] The article is entitled "Christianity and Human Rights."

this comes solicitude for the weak, the unsuccessful, and the unhappy. From pity grew the medieval concept of chivalry, which entailed special obligations toward women and others in society who lacked brute strength; from pity also springs most of our modern "social consciousness."

In summarizing at some length Miss Ward's article, I do not mean to suggest that the "democratic countries" are paragons of Christian virtue, or even that their citizens are aware that their attitudes have been shaped by Christianity. But it does seem clear that the attitudes, though often expressed in secular language, come mostly from the many centuries of religious faith and teaching that lie back of modern political developments. How long the attitudes will survive with the decline in the faith that gave them birth, I shall not try to answer. A cut flower will keep its freshness in water for many days, but in time it withers.

However, if post-modern civilization does turn out to be Christian, the psychological foundations of democracy will be strongly reinforced. Democracy will become once more, as it was originally, one of the more useful by-products of Christianity.

~ 7 ~

The Underloved

In any society there are certain groups that are singled out for discrimination or are irrationally disliked by the dominant majority—or dominant minority. The term "underprivileged" has been freely bandied about in recent years as a convenient label, but it sounds too impersonal, suggesting little more than the rear position in a cafeteria line. I propose to speak instead of the "underloved," some of whom have adequate bank accounts but still find a social wall erected around them. The two classifications do not entirely overlap.

Several of these groups I shall treat briefly, because I doubt that Christianity would do much more than support and accelerate the best tendencies now evident in secular thinking about them. Such is the case with the problem of criminals, lunatics, and the very poor, who, taken together, form a large block of the population which is punished, protected (or a little of both) by the paid functionaries of society.

Of the three groups, the criminals fare best. They are handled with a matter-of-factness which leaves them some shreds of dignity. Their private lives are not as inquisitively probed as those of the very poor, and the prisons in which they are confined are usually more humane than insane asylums.

This is not to say that nothing further would need to be done in a Christian society. The final aim (which would never be completely achieved) would be to abolish crime altogether by eliminating the social and psychological conditions that cause it. Much would depend on the economic system developed by the new society. If differences in wealth were evened up so that the poor were not constantly tempted by the sight of ostentatious riches, and if a genuine opportunity were provided for everyone to earn a decent living by creatively satisfying work, fewer men would be pushed into crime by envy, hunger, and frustration.

Many crimes, however, arise from subtle psychological sources. This is seen especially in juvenile delinquents who often steal or murder not for gain but because crime provides an ersatz pattern to life. The excitement of defying society and the camaraderie of sharing dangers with other rebels can invest crime with almost a moral aura. Christianity banishes the need of a self-made pattern, for it is the magic link between things that are otherwise parts of a chaotic whole: it gives a sense of over-all meaning to everything from the solar system to the molecules inside the body; it destroys the aching vacuum of aimlessness.

A better society and more Christianity in the air would reduce crime, but not eliminate it altogether. There would still be the problem of what to do with the specific offender brought before the court. Here, I do not see how the most Christian judge and jury could do more or better than the best judges and juries do now: balance the safety of society against the welfare of the criminal, and decide whether they are justified in gambling on his reformation by imposing a suspended sentence or whether a more drastic punishment is necessary. However, if the number of malefactors were smaller and court dockets less crowded, more time could be devoted to individual cases, with the result that the use of parole, suspended sentence, etc., would more often be practical than it is during a period when crime flourishes on a mass-production level.

One thing a Christian society could do—treat the criminal's family with something other than the barbaric neglect which is now usually its lot. A woman whose husband is imprisoned is a woman whose husband is temporarily dead. To drive her to prostitution or drudgery is to punish her rather than him; the savagery of the totalitarian "group punishments" is not morally more indefensible than this. The prisoner's family should be aided as generously and unhumiliatingly as are the blind, the crippled, and widowed mothers.

Christianity's greatest impact might be on the criminal after he is confined in prison. It is true that most prisons today have chaplains, but the general atmosphere both in prison and without is so colored by the philosophy of "getting ahead" and "devil take the hindermost" that the most devoted chaplain has an uphill job. He must combat not only the criminal tendencies of the men whom he tries to help, but the not dissimilar attitudes of the respectable citizens roaming at large.

More Christianity in the air would facilitate a religious approach. I do not anticipate wholesale conversions and reformations, but there are definite advantages to the religious approach, and it would sometimes succeed where nothing else would. Christianity offers the criminal two things that he needs—whether or not he consciously realizes the need. First of all, it teaches him that in most cases he has not merely been "antisocial." He has *sinned*. He has quarreled not with society but with God. When he finishes his sentence, he has "paid his debt to society," but he has not righted his relationship toward God. This realization, of course, leads to a deeper sense of guilt, which would make the criminal's problem worse than before if it were not for Christianity's second contribution: the forgiveness of sins. The criminal needs this just as his judge and jurors need it. Society cannot forgive sins; it can only punish crimes and balance the books. Only God, by accepting repentance and granting unqualified forgiveness, can really wipe the slate clean.

Since the time of Jeremy Bentham and even earlier, a great number of humanitarians have labored with some success to improve the treatment of criminals. At present, as witnessed by several recent novels and factual studies, the plight of lunatics is coming to the fore. The condition of most lunatics, as revealed by many dispassionate investigators, is so degrading that the power of the English language—blunt and plain-spoken as it is—falls short of expressing the full horror. Many of the public asylums, and some of the private ones, would fit without change in one of the inner circles of Dante's "Inferno." The attendants are almost always underpaid and are frequently maladjusted to the point of sadism. The helplessness of the inmates encourages any latent brutality in their keepers. The asylums themselves are often cold dungeons, underheated because of the legislature's love of the taxpayer. The food is not always up to the level of postwar Germany. Many an asylum delights casual passers-by with its façade of pleasant white columns and neat flower beds on the lawn, but one remembers the whited sepulcher.

The ideal solution for insanity, as for crime, is to prevent it. The best that a Christian society will realistically hope for is not to prevent it altogether but to reduce its frequency by counteracting the psychological conditions that are often the main reason for mental derangement.

The truth is that insanity is today a logical reaction to the futile picture of the universe offered by thoroughgoing atheism. The modern, if he is intelligent enough to turn philosopher, typically sees around him a completely meaningless world. The stars move in their courses, but they are not interested in him. Unseen, the tireless, sinister atoms whirl in his body. He has impulses—to eat, drink, copulate, write detective stories, play the oboe—and these impulses have no visible connection with stars or atoms. Meanwhile he grows older day by day. His visits to the dentist are more frequent; soon it will be time for a partial denture. Soon he and his denture will be underground and quickly forgotten by other men growing old and having dentures made. And the sun itself is growing old, and someday the earth will be a globe of ice, and that is all there is to it.

The psychologist Jung, after dealing with thousands of neurotics, reported that without exception one fundamental problem of all his patients over thirty-five was the need for an adequate religious viewpoint. Christianity gives a satisfying, almost dramatic, meaning to life. Every individual is loved by the supreme power of the universe and can turn to that power for help. Regardless of the teeth that decay and the eyes that fail here on earth, the individual can begin now to enter into the inexpressible life of fulfillment that will be his permanently. When God is put in the center, the cosmic jigsaw puzzle fits together.

Insanity should decline once the universe begins to make sense. But what of the irreducible number of lunatics? Christianity, I think, would lead to two changes in dealing with them. For one thing, there would be less indecent haste to shunt the mildly deranged off to the nearest institution. If society becomes more decentralized, it should be possible to let many harmless half-wits roam at liberty. (In a large

city, of course, the automobile makes their presence a
hazard.) I am thinking of a small New England village
which has a locally famous half-wit. Everyone, from the
selectmen to young children, takes a benevolent interest in
Willie (not his real name), looks after him, and proudly
points him out to visitors. Willie works at odd jobs, has a
shack which is his castle, goes wherever he pleases. When
an impulse seizes him to string twine between the trees so
that they can converse with one another, he does so. His
appearance is uncouth and would distress the villagers if
they believed that all citizens should be as neat as the
lawns and gardens they so lovingly tend. But they feel
nothing of the sort. Willie to them is a human being toward
whom they have special obligations. One senses that in this
small village there survives something of the ancient
Christian feeling that mental defectives are the "innocents
of God." Or it may be that the villagers unconsciously
recall that Christ showed special compassion for sinners, the
sick, and the demented—the elements of society that contribute least to the prestige and tidiness of the community.

Perhaps Willie would be better off in an institution, if it
were the right kind. His diet would be better balanced, his
hair cut more often. Perhaps . . . But one may doubt
whether greater neatness and more vitamins would make
up, in his eyes, for loss of freedom. At any rate, he would
not be better off in most asylums, as they exist at this writing.

I have been speaking of borderline cases. Obviously,
some lunatics must be locked up for their own protection or
that of society. Here I think Christianity would result in
a drastic sharpening of the public conscience and loosening
of purse strings. "Out of sight, out of mind" is incompatible
with Christianity. A Christian society will be obligated to
spend money on a lavish scale to provide the most humane

and expert treatment for this class of people who, of all, are the most helpless and innocent victims of misfortune.

Vying with lunatics for the title of the most unfortunate are the people receiving public charity or relief. They are subjected to the trained attention of an army of social workers who enter their homes with a sheaf of questionnaires and probing inquisitiveness.

It would be cruel and unjust to disparage en masse the great army of social workers. They serve a necessary function in a fiercely competitive society, being indispensable to tidy up the back alleys when the stench begins to stifle the residents in the better parts of town. Theirs is a well-nigh impossible assignment. Many of them heroically strive to remain human and compassionate in the midst of their crushing responsibilities. Others are beaten down by the sheer volume of the misery about them, and soon begin to feel that the people they help are nothing but eating and breeding machines, one scarcely distinguishable from the next in their common grayness.

In a Christian society, relief work should be handled on the local level whenever possible. (Clearly, this would not be practical in time of great natural disasters or serious depressions; I am thinking of the inevitable amount of welfare work required in normal years.) The advantage of this is that the actual facts of each case can be ascertained in a more human, neighborly way, and aid can be given with fewer questionnaires. Many of the churches would probably rediscover their ancient obligation to care for any of their members who become destitute. In modern times the Mormons have shown that it is possible for a church to do this. In the very midst of the depression the Mormons, by establishing group canneries, etc., cared for their people and kept them off relief. The gain in self-respect and morale needs no comment.

Public relief work needs to be infused with religious assumptions if the material good it accomplishes is not more than counterbalanced by the psychological harm. Training schools for social workers will very likely find that courses in theology and Christian ethics are as indispensable to their students as lectures in techniques. The welfare worker, dealing with human souls as well as bodies, has as delicate a task as the surgeon performing a brain operation. One would consider a surgeon poorly prepared if he knew everything about surgical knives and anesthesia and nothing about the structure of the brain.

The value of religious motivation in relief work is illustrated by the long history of the Quakers. They have been consistently successful in aiding the unfortunate and restoring their self-respect at the same time. Their welfare missions are greeted anywhere in the world with unmixed gratitude, because the people who are aided by them sense that outgoing love, not rational and cold duty, motivates the Friends.

I have up to now spoken of various classes of 'people who are the wards of society. What Christianity would produce in regard to them would not be a complete revolution but extensive reforms, both in attitude and methods. I come now to a very different group—racial minorities. Very different because the criminal can reform, the lunatic can regain his sanity, and the destitute man rise to prosperity, but the Negro or Chinese cannot change his skin. And there is another difference. The Christian viewpoint on racial problems involves not reform but revolution.

Of the racial minorities in America, the Negroes constitute the largest group and the one subject to the most spectacular humiliations and cruelty. Whenever America embarks on one of its self-righteous campaigns to give good advice to the world, the world grinningly inquires,

"What about the Negroes in Mississippi and Detroit?" Sound instinct dictates that the Negro should be regarded as the touchstone for America's protestations of virtue.

The problem we have inherited is an excellent example of evil accumulating mountain-high without any deep-dyed villains consciously willing it. Negro slavery in America developed almost casually in the course of the seventeenth century. The slaves, useful for household work and farm labor, were scarcely worse off than the white indentured servants. Hardly anyone dreamed of defending the system as a permanent social institution. The great men of the American Revolution—Washington, Jefferson, Madison, Hamilton, Patrick Henry, and others—condemned it; many of them emancipated their own slaves and felt sure that the whole system would soon wither away.

It probably would have but for that catastrophic day in 1794 when Eli Whitney patented the cotton gin. Cotton became big money. Slaves were available as cheap labor for the cotton plantations. Human nature, which might have resisted the lure of small profits, could not stand up against the temptation of potential wealth. Plantation slavery on a grand scale, and frequently organized with the impersonal efficiency of large factories, spread like an ugly sore over the South.

The Civil War is sometimes explained as nothing more than a struggle between the industrial North and the agrarian South, as though the Northerners with their monkey wrenches went forth to battle the Southerners with their pitchforks. That economic factors accentuated the hostility of the two sections, no one will deny. But it demands a doctrinaire faith in Economic Man to believe that the guns would have started firing if the slavery issue had not been the basic one. (If economics were the sole cause of the Civil War, the South and West would today be conducting military operations against the Northeast in order to overthrow the network of discriminatory freight rates by which the latter exploits the rest of the country. Instead, the injustice is being fought out and remedied in the Supreme Court.) The real economic factor in the Civil War was the development of the plantation system and the consequent expansion of slavery; in other words, an economic event resulted in a moral problem, and the moral problem resulted in war.

The abolition movement at first encountered almost as much resistance in the North as in the South. The conservatives looked upon it with dubious eyes; they were not anxious to upset the applecart. The movement itself can be understood only as the long-delayed fruits of the Christian doctrine of the Fatherhood of God and the Brotherhood of Man. The abolitionist leaders, whether church members or not, were reared in a civilization shot through and through with Christian assumptions. Too many people over too many centuries had read the Bible, listened to sermons on brotherhood, and meditated on the fact that Christ died for *all* men, for the clear denial of Christianity implicit in slavery to be forever overlooked. It is true that the New Testament does not forbid slavery, but it commands slave and master to regard each other as brothers. Since this cannot be done when one wields the hoe and the other the cat-o'-nine-tails, the only remedy was to get rid of slavery.

In reality, the connection between the abolition movement and Christianity was much more direct than I have suggested above. The movement did not really get under way on a large scale and win over large numbers of supporters until after the religious revival of 1830; several of the most effective revivalists of that period became abolitionist leaders, and the fervor of religious enthusiasm generated by the Revival was inseparably associated with abolitionism in the minds of many church leaders and converts.[1]

After the Civil War was over and the slaves had been constitutionally emancipated, most abolitionists sat back with the contented feeling that the job was done. The South was busy licking its wounds; the North was breeding robber barons to exploit the advancing frontier; the Republican party was degenerating from the party of Lincoln to the party of Grant. Few observers noticed that the Negroes were now neither free men nor slaves. An amendment to the Constitution does not solve all problems.

In the South, the characteristic system of voting restrictions, separate schools, antimiscegenation laws, and general segregation developed. In the North, matters were handled in more genteel fashion. Discrimination, though almost equally galling, was embodied not so much in laws as in social customs which evolved and hardened in the great cities as Negroes began drifting northward from the devastated South. As far as possible, the whites herded the new arrivals into the slums and kept them out of sight. Occasional riots broke out along the frontiers between white and Negro sections. Popular song writers, half amused and half hostile, celebrated the influx of the Negroes in such lyrics as "Rufus Rastus Johnson Brown, watchu gonna do when the rent comes 'round?" The minstrel show, which antedated the Civil War, continued to present the black man as the eternal child.

The minstrel show and the comic songs about Negroes have almost disappeared today—a negative sign that the long complacency is ending. More positive indications are

[1] This whole question is discussed with abundant documentation by Gilbert Hobbs Barnes in his book, *The Antislavery Impulse: 1830-1844* (New York & London: D. Appleton-Century Co., 1933).

the establishment of interracial committees; the efforts of many schools to teach mutual understanding; the immense number of books on Negro problems; the enlightened attitude of some labor unions; the improvement of Negro schools in the South; and the great decrease in the frequency of lynchings.

America is now in the second wave of conscience. Like the first which culminated in legal emancipation, the real driving force is the inherited insights of Christianity plus the never completely dormant moral sense inside each person. But the temper of the times renders a frankly religious approach difficult, and compels many reformers— whatever their personal beliefs—to phrase their pleas in the forbidding "gobbledegook" of quasi science.

In pamphlets and from the platform we are urged to improve the lot of the Negroes because they are the same as other people, except for biologically minor characteristics like dark skin and curly hair. We are shown elaborate statistics to confute the idea that all Negroes have low I.Q.'s; biographies of outstanding Negroes are published to prove that they can equal the whites in genius and drive.

This kind of reasoning has one serious drawback. It contains no answer to the irrational motives that inspire most race prejudice. What can the biologist say to the heckler who shouts, "What you say is all very well, but I don't *like* black skin and woolly hair!"? If he answers "You shouldn't let these little physical differences keep you from behaving decently toward another human," he ceases to speak as a scientist and enters the province of the philosopher, moralist, and priest. Science is concerned with facts, not values.

Christianity makes an absolute approach to racial problems possible. The universalistic note of Christ's teachings is revealed repeatedly in the Gospels, nowhere more

emphatically than in His last recorded words: "Go ye therefore, and teach all nations, baptizing them in the name of
the Father, and of the Son, and of the Holy Ghost; Teaching them to observe all things whatsoever I have commanded you: and, lo, I am with you alway, even unto the
end of the world. Amen."

However, it is unnecessary to hunt out "proof texts."
Christ's constant emphasis on the Fatherhood of God is
sufficient. Paul in his turn deliberately leaps across the
greatest barrier of his time—that between Jews and Gentiles.
"Is he the God of the Jews only? Is he not also of the
Gentiles? Yes, of the Gentiles also." In Athens he stood on
Mars' Hill and proclaimed that God "hath made of one
blood all nations of men." From beginning to end, the
teachings and implications of the New Testament point to
only one categorical conclusion: knock down all barriers.
After the time has come when Negroes, Caucasians, and
Chinese can glance at one another as casually as a blue-eyed
Caucasian observes a brown-eyed Caucasian, a Christian
attitude toward race may be said to prevail.

There is nothing in "human nature" to prevent this.
Racial differences in Argentina and Brazil constitute relatively slight barriers. But in America there is an untold
amount of inertia and violent opposition to overcome. The
spearhead of the force to overcome racial barriers ought to
be, and can be, the churches.

If the churches undertake this they will be living in
glasshouses. They must first eliminate any vestiges of segregation in their own organization. Good progress in this
direction has already been made by a number of denominations. But more than this—the ancient prophetic function
falls upon the churches: to teach and preach day in and

day out that God is the God of justice, and that a Jim Crow society is by definition unjust.

There may be withdrawals of financial support, shrinkages in membership, even martyrdoms at the hands of mobs. Such consequences are of no importance. The Church, being divinely established, need fear nothing except its own apostasy. In the long run, uncompromising Christianity will win over the men of good will, and the loss of nominal Christians will not be reckoned an unmixed misfortune.

A living Christianity which refused to recognize any compartments of life sealed off from Christianity would greatly accelerate the gradual amelioration of racial relations which is now observable. It would be the peculiar task of the Church never to let society rest on its oars; to goad it on whenever a comfortable compromise seemed to have been reached.

Certain injustices would wither away more easily than others. Even today the average white man is not too much opposed to increased educational and occupational opportunities for Negroes. More deeply embedded in social habits are the various types of segregation—Jim Crow cars, zoning restrictions, separate schools, etc. But they, too, are barriers, and must go. The final question is the one always shouted by the anti-Negro rabble-rouser: "Would all this lead to intermarriage?"

The Christian answer is: Yes, if individual Negroes and whites wished it. Christianity cannot knock down all other barriers and leave this one standing. Whether such marriages will take place on a large scale is doubtful, at least for a considerable future. Certainly as long as any vestige of racial antagonism survives in either race, a mixed marriage involves strains additional to those inherent in any marriage. The same thing holds for marriages between people of different religions, from different economic groups, or with different interests.

But these are immediate and "practical" considerations. During the transition period when race prejudice is slowly eroding, some Negroes and whites, quite simply falling in love, will choose to brave the extra difficulties. The sincere Christian can only wish them well and help them meet any obstacles that spring up along their way.

I fear I have been speaking as though a nation of white people, suddenly illumined by Christian faith, decided to do something for their colored brethren. Such an attitude would be both condescending and unrealistic. The whites would be doing even more for themselves. No one can calculate the amount of psychological and spiritual harm that Negro-haters and Negro-fearers inflict upon themselves. A double standard in race relations is as death-dealing as in sex relations; it leads to intellectual dishonesty and severe emotional conflicts barely beneath the surface. The Negroes were legally emancipated by the Civil War. The steady pressure of Christianity could complete their emancipation. And with its completion, the white race in America would also be emancipated.

It would be possible now to go on and discuss in detail the other racial minorities in America, such as the Japanese, Chinese, and Mexicans, but what I have said about the Negroes should apply—*mutatis mutandis*—to them. Instead of repeating most of the things I have said, I should like to deal briefly with a "racial" group which occupies a somewhat different position: the Jews.

I put "racial" in quotation marks, for anyone who has ever been with a dozen Jews at one time knows that practically every racial strain of Europe and western Asia has entered into their blood. There is no such thing as a typical Jew, any more than there is a typical American. The Jews are not a race but a "religio-cultural group."

It is easy to assume that anti-Semitism is based on religious prejudice, but the evidence is against this. One anti-Semite will say he hates the Jews because they murdered Christ, but the next one, an atheist, hates them because Christ was a Jew. The religious theory particularly breaks down when an occasional Jew embraces Christianity and still finds himself blackballed by anti-Semitic "Christians" at the country club.

The Jews were widely dispersed over the Roman Empire long before the time of Christ, and were the objects of widespread hostility and persecution. Tacitus (A.D. ca. 55-ca.120) who was anything but a Christian, loathed the Jews. He hated them because they were different. They had no images of their God; they practiced circumcision; they refused to intermarry with Gentiles; they wouldn't eat what others considered good food; they disapproved of the fine old Roman habit of infanticide.[2]

After the rationalizations, which vary with times and individuals, are stripped away, *differentness* emerges as the real motive for the irrational hostility the Jews have had to endure off and on for over two thousand years.

They began being different long before the year A.D. 1. Instead of worshiping Baal and Moloch like other people, they insisted on serving a God who was so peculiar that He permitted no one to make images of Him. The Jews were the torchbearers of monotheism for centuries while the rest of the world worshiped devils, supermen, and philosophic abstractions. If a man has been a torchbearer

[2] For a full presentation of Tacitus' prejudices in his own words, see Tacitus, *The Histories*, translated by Clifford H. Moore (Cambridge: Harvard University Press), vol. II, Loeb Classical Library, pp. 177 ff.

for a long time, his arms get in the habit of holding a torch. He continues to hold it, even when other men (Christians and Mohammedans) begin carrying somewhat similar torches.

The Jews, having been the custodians of religious truth for centuries, became specialized. It is in their blood, so to speak, to bear unending witness to the only true God. This does not mean that they deny that the Christian God and the Mohammedan Allah are also the one true God—they gladly admit it—but the sense of a special mission remains, interwoven with national memories, special customs, and a strong group feeling.

This partly explains, but does not justify, the prejudices of many Gentiles. The task of the Christian community is to overcome the irrational herd instinct which hates and fears anything that is different. If the Jews, having a long and special history, wish to remain a cultural and religious group maintained by marriage within the group, that is their right; it is then up to their Christian neighbors to show that this need constitute no barrier to "neighborliness." The Brotherhood of Man is not a closed corporation; it is not confined to fellow believers.

The Church in its teachings could do much to drive home the fact that Judaism is the mother, or at least the matrix of Christianity. Had the Jews not prepared the way, the ancient world would have been utterly unable to understand what happened at Bethlehem and Calvary. The New Testament is incomprehensible without the Old. And Christ, the Saviour and incarnate God of Christinity, was born of a Jewish mother. All of these things combine to give any thoughtful Christian a feeling of gratitude, almost of reverence, toward the Jews as a people. In one sense, all Christians *are* Jews already for Christianity has taken over Jewish monotheism, the Jewish moral teachings, and the Jewish Old Testament. The disgraceful friction between Jews and Christians is not the quarrel of complete strangers but the less excusable backbiting between close relatives.

The churches will need to fight anti-Semitism in the abstract, and also in its specific manifestations. Restrictive covenants, quotas in colleges, all-Gentile clubs, discrimination in employment opportunities—all must and will be done away with if Christians dare discover what their religion means by love and brotherhood.

It would be easy to stop at this point, but I must add one thing more. No Christian is permitted to let differences in religion separate him from his "neighbor," but he can and must hope that in the fullness of time all neighbors will become Christian. The direct command of Christ that His teachings should be carried to "all nations" is sufficient authority, and the tenor of all Christian thought is in keeping with this.

Christianity itself is split into hundreds of sects. All of these ought to be reunited into the one universal Church. But earlier than the divisions and subdivisions of the Church there occurred the break between Judaism and early Christianity. Only when that split is healed can the Christian feel that the Church is fully reunited.

Such is the ultimate hope and prayer of any Christian who takes the words of Christ seriously. But this hope must not be allowed to stand in the way of Christ's equally emphatic teaching, "Thou shalt love thy neighbor as thyself." The spirit of Christianity forbids shrewd bargaining. No one is permitted to say, "Be baptized, and then we'll be neighbors."

It is the other way around. When Christians at last show by deeds as well as words that they are neighbors, the individual Jew can accept or reject Christianity according as he believes it true or false—and without having his decision influenced by unpleasant emotional associations. And the individual Christian will have the same freedom: if he decides that Judaism is true and Christianity a false addition, he should embrace Judaism. There is only one valid reason for adhering to a particular religion: belief that it is true.

This chapter, I imagine, contains very little that thoughtful Christians would controvert, no matter how reluctant they might be to confront some of the logical conclusions of Christianity. If you find yourself stopping short at some points, do not be surprised. In several places (I shall not say where) I had to force myself to go on. Inherited habits of thought and feeling were pulling me back; an all too familiar voice was whispering in my ear: "Let's be reasonable and practical; this is a good point at which to stabilize things." That voice has no doubt been whispering to you, though perhaps not at the same places. No two people have assimilated precisely the same inhibitions and prejudices.

But I am afraid that Christianity is something that the individual and his society have to see through to the end. None of us will like everything that we can foresee at the end of the road. We have our quirks, our pet dislikes, which we should like to carry along. They don't take up much room in our luggage, and we are sure they wouldn't get in anyone's way. But we can't. This is one of the best proofs that Christianity was not invented by any mere human. If it were, it would completely satisfy an occasional individual. Instead, the shoe pinches somewhere at some time with everyone. At least that is what I am keenly aware of as I finish this chapter.

8

Beyond the Nation

In most of the chapters up to this point I have had the United States and its particular problems in mind. But to write of one nation as though it occupied a planet unto itself is to fall into archaic ruts of thinking. Thanks to the two World Wars there is now a blessed lack of controversy about the interdependence of all nations, except in the surviving pockets of the isolationist belt.

When world relations are examined in the light of Christianity, the conclusions are clear-cut. Christians must agree with the one-worlders: world government, federally organized, is the goal. The Christian attitude is, of course, based on belief in the Brotherhood of Man, but this in itself would not necessitate world government if railways, steamboats, airplanes, radio, atomic bombs, and guided missiles were nonexistent. A primitive technology limits the contacts between peoples, limits their power to aid one another or to harm one another. World government becomes practical and necessary only when technology is highly advanced—as it is today. Almost the whole globe is as accessible to the merchant and tourist as were the provinces of the Roman Empire twenty centuries ago. Human nature being the explosive thing it is, the contacts will lead either to world co-operation or world war. There is no longer a middle ground.

If Christianity agrees with the program of the secular one-worlders, does it have any additional comments to make? I think it does. It can help distinguish between what is essential and what is optional in a world federation.

For example, Christianity refuses to regard economics as the basis of everything else. In this it parts company with classical laissez-faire capitalism and Marxist communism. Wall Street can keep its exchanges and Moscow its commissars, provided (and this is essential) that neither capitalism nor communism is elevated into an absolute. Two systems of idolatry cannot co-operate; Moloch and Baal will demand blood sacrifices.

The doctrinaire Communists, confronting doctrinaire capitalists, see this clearly. So long as the thought habits of modern man are geared first and foremost to economic theories, so that all else—philosophy, religion, art, ethics— seems a mere by-product of who-gets-what, the competing systems are destined to settle their competition on the battle-field. The only way the economic *ism's* can exist peacefully in the same world is to regard them as pragmatic and pro-visional arrangements for particular social conditions. They must be looked upon as secondary—a lesson that Communists and capitalists have still to learn.

Something must be primary. There must be a set of principles or attitudes or beliefs that goes deeper than economics and can provide a feeling of unity, however diverse the economic and political systems of the world.

The primary thing is something so obvious that the mention of it smacks of a platitude. It is a belief in the fixed and absolute moral order of the universe—a moral order which is not merely a reflection of class interests, not merely a rule-of-thumb collection of maxims worked out by society to avoid friction. The moral order simply *is*. One may disobey it, but one may·not alter it.

The moral law, as taught by almost all great religons and philosophies, consists of the familiar commandments of fair play: treating other people as one would be treated, loving one's neighbor as oneself. If these absolutes are replaced by "social expediency," the next and easy step is for each individual or group to be expedient for its own private aims. Social expediency is hopelessly subjective; in practice it means that the strong men or strong nations identify their selfish interests with the larger welfare and complacently order the rest of the world around.

Most cultures, even seemingly primitive ones, have had this concept of the fixed moral order. It remained for liberal Western civilization to weaken it, and for the bastard children of the West—fascism and communism—to carry the repudiation a step further. Today the corrosive acids distilled in liberal England and America and totalitarian Germany and Russia are at work in Asia, eating away at the ancient concepts of moral law there and clearing a path for the advance of "social expediency"—with inevitable abuses by the men at the top.

If Western civilization distilled the poison, it has the opportunity to produce the antidote. For a long time to come the exchange of ideas between the Orient and the Occident will probably still run heavily in the Occident-to-Orient direction. In consequence of this, any strengthening of the concept of moral absolutes in Europe and the New World will counteract the corrosion now obvious in Asia.

Christianity, if it springs into new life, will provide the antidote in Western civilization. Does this mean that the rest of the world must also become Christian? Does world government depend on the Mohammedans, Buddhists, Hindus, and Confucianists accepting Christianity?

I do not think it does. If members of other religious groups find in their faiths the same moral and social atti- tudes that are implicit in Christianity, the basis may be adequate. To say this is not to deny that the basis would be stronger if Christianity became the universal religion. Fantastic as it sounds, the possibility must not be ruled out. Professor Toynbee has shown that of the half-a-dozen living civilizations, our own—despite its sickly state—has still the greatest vitality. And in so far as it possesses a genuine religion, that religion is Christianity, and Christianity is the only large-scale faith fired with a strong missionary impulse. In almost every country there are Christian out- posts. Assuming that the decay of other cultures is not arrested, and that, at the same time, Christianity experi- ences one of its periodic bursts of new vitality, the prophecy of Toynbee may come true:[1]

Our modern Western secular civilization in its turn may serve its historical purpose by providing Christianity with a com- pletely world-wide repetition of the Roman Empire to spread over. . . . long before a world is unified politically, it is unified economically and in other material ways; and the unification of our present world has long since opened the way for St. Paul, who once travelled from the Orontes to the Tiber under the aegis of the *Pax Romana,* to travel on from the Tiber to the Mississippi and from the Mississippi to the Yangtse; while Clement's and Origen's work of infusing Greek philosophy into Christianity at Alexandria might be emulated in some city of the Far East by the infusion of Chinese philosophy into Christi- anity. . . . It is even possible that as, under the Roman Empire, Christianity drew out of and inherited from the other Oriental

---

[1] Arnold J. Toynbee, "Christianity and Civilization," *Civilization on Trial* (New York: Oxford University Press, 1948), pp. 239-40. Quoted by permission of the publishers.

religions the heart of what was best in them, so the present religions of India and the form of Buddhism that is practised to-day in the Far East may contribute new elements to be grafted onto Christianity in days to come. . . . Christianity may be left as the spiritual heir of all the other higher religions, from the post-Sumerian rudiment of one in the worship of Tammuz and Ishtar down to those that in A.D. 1948 are still living separate lives side by side with Christianity, and of all the philosophies from Ikhnaton's to Hegel's. . . .

Even if the miracle does not occur, Christianity seems certain to have a profound effect on other religions. To some extent this has already happened. Gandhi was not a Christian, but he was so deeply under the influence of Christ and the New Testament that he was (from the Christian viewpoint) at least a fellow traveler. In the Moslem countries where converts have been extremely few, large numbers of Mohammedans educated in mission schools have absorbed more of the Christian outlook than they realize. Indirect Christian influence in China is still more marked.

There is no reason why the traffic need be one way. In fact, there is now a small but valuable volume of reverse lend-lease. The neo-mystic movement, centered in California but largely of Oriental genesis, is today making thoughful Christians re-examine the mystical strain in their own faith. One can easily think of other values implicit in Christianity but needing to be brought out in the open by the explicit teachings of different religions. For example, the Buddhist doctrines of right vocation and compassion toward animals are thoroughly in the Christian spirit, and many professing Christians could profitably study the Moslems' passionate conviction of the utter reality of Allah's presence and majesty, as well as the Moslem application of the principle of brotherhood in racial relations.

Short of world-wide Christianization, the most hopeful

possibility is therefore the enriching contact of the various religions, so that each finds all its buried treasures brought to the surface by the others. This does not mean a melting-pot faith; there is a hard core of Christian dogma, centered around the Incarnation and the Atonement, which forbids any effort to equate Christianity with plain "religion." But as each religion comes to realize its own resources, understanding should increase rather than decrease. The more Christian a man is, the more he has in common with the Buddhist, Mohammedan, and Jew. It is the complete secularist who has almost nothing in common with anyone else.

But back to the question of moral absolutes. However the belief is achieved, it is essential. When codified for political use, it results in a doctrine of inalienable rights similar to that of the American Declaration of Independence and the first ten amendments to the federal Constitution. This is not parochial thinking; the founding fathers were so steeped in the concept of moral absolutes that they naturally embodied them in their political formulations. But, joined to belief in inalienable rights, the world will be obliged to develop the companion concept of essential duties. The easy tendency to talk endlessly about rights and never about duties leads swiftly to glorified selfishness, such as prevailed in America during the robber-baron era and yet lurks in dark corners.

Belief in the absolute moral order, and derived from that belief a set of "inalienable rights" and "necessary duties"— such is the psychological basis of world federation. The rest is common sense. Only the turn that history takes can determine whether a world federation can be organized in one stroke or must evolve from the union of those nations that share the essential basis, and then gradually receive other nations as their peoples become willing to accept the underlying assumptions.

World federation does not mean world uniformity. If this were fully grasped, many of the vehement (and valid) objections would disappear. There is no reason why the Chinese and Americans should eat the same breakfast foods or wear the same cut of clothes; Europe can cling to the chromatic scale and the Hindus keep their quarter-tones. One world need not speak one language.

This last point is worth a moment's elaboration, since it symbolizes the principle of diversity-within-unity. Unity requires that the diplomats, missionaries, tourists, and businessmen of every country have some easy way of talking together, and that scientists be able to publish their discoveries without the prohibitive cost of innumerable translations. The problem can be easily solved by adopting a simple "artificial language" such as Esperanto and having it taught in all the secondary schools of the world. It need not and should not supplant the national tongues. These would remain the favorites of the creative writer, the orator, and the lover. Indeed the adoption of an international language would give a new lease on life to many splendid tongues, such as Welsh and Provençal, which have been pushed into the background because of the need for communicating with people from larger language areas. The Welshman could cultivate his Welsh as a literary language and speak Esperanto when he went to London.

This solicitude for small language groups and local customs has a Christian, not a romantic, basis. Just as God created both the blue jay and the goldfinch, and each has a beauty that is different from the other's, so there are things that can be said in Welsh but not in English—and vice versa. And local habits—courtship customs, dances, celebrations, etc.—are with rare exceptions good in themselves. There is no reason why every county should be the same any more than every person should be the same.

The modern nation-state is the enemy of both the county and the world. It enters into rivalry with other nation-states and menaces the peace of the world; it overwhelms the local customs of the county and creates the dreary standardized civilization one finds in so many countries—in America, the uniform filling stations, the identical hotels with identical menus, the dime stores with indistinguishable façades from Maine to Oregon.

The religious impulse toward variety had free rein during the Middle Ages, when nearly every village possessed some distinctive custom or turn of phrase to make it memorable. There was also the spirit, if not the fact, of an all-embracing unity—provided by Christianity and the Church. Where the Middle Ages failed was in not translating the spirit of unity into a political fact. Medieval wars, while far less bloody than modern ones, were as numerous. If the modern world can create the spirit of unity, based on agreement in regard to basic values, and then incarnate it in a world federation, it will succeed where the Middle Ages failed. But there is no short cut. The world today is the temple of many varieties of idol worship—capitalism, communism, etc.—and until the idols are overthrown by a change of heart on the part of their worshipers, the blood sacrifices will be offered up.

Perhaps what I have so far written suggests utopian thinking; I may have given the impression that a mysterious force is irresistibly moving the nations toward world federation. The force of logic certainly points in that direction, but man —being a creature with free will—has the privilege of disregarding logic and choosing to think with his blood or anything else. The Christian, like everyone else, must reckon with the possibility that national sovereignty will continue for an indefinite future to be the nemesis of the world. And if this is so, the likelihood of war—and what to do about it —is not to be evaded.

The churches here speak with a divided voice. There are certain denominations, such as the Mennonites and the Quakers, which have historically and consistently insisted on pacifism, often at the cost of severe persecution. The majority of churches have not been officially pacifist, though almost without exception they have faced the question of war with troubled consciences and number among their members a sizable group of pacifists.

The controversy between pacifists and nonpacifists does not involve any dispute over whether war is a good thing: all Christians know that it is detestable. Nor can the disagreement be settled by appeal to the unambiguous teachings of Christ. In this regard, the problem is quite different from the question of marriage and divorce. Christ stated his doctrine of matrimony with ruthless clarity, and the Church need be in no doubt as to its Founder's commands, except in a few borderline situations. But nowhere in the recorded sayings of Christ does he deal directly with the Christian's duty in time of war. It is true that the general emphasis of His teaching was on love and turning the other cheek. However, it must be remembered that He also said we should render unto Caesar the things that are Caesar's; that in His relations with the Roman centurion he passed up the opportunity to rebuke him for his sanguinary profession; and that when He decided to cleanse the Temple he resorted to the violent expedient of wielding a whip. If on any occasion Christ said a definite Yes or No to the question of participation in war, his words have not been preserved in the Gospel records. It is therefore impossible to underline a particular verse in the New Testament and say, "That settles it."

The pacifist case, as I understand it, rests on the general spirit of Christ's teachings—returning good for evil, loving the world into goodness. The nonpacifist contends that the attempt to apply these teachings literally in all phases of group life overlooks the valid distinction between the actions of the individual and those of the group. The problems connected with the latter are never simple. To give one example: It might have been ultra-Christian for an individual German Christian to turn the other cheek when a member of the S.S. slapped him (though even here some qualifications are perhaps called for), but if England as a whole had turned her national cheek to Nazi Germany one might have questioned whether she was behaving in a Christian way toward the inhabitants of the Nazi concentration camps. In other words, the nonpacifist, while hating war, sees pacifism as an oversimplification of reality—and consequently no automatic solution.

The recent world meeting of churches at Amsterdam officially recognized both viewpoints as validly Christian. It is a great pity that Christians cannot agree on a problem of such importance, but it would be dishonest to pretend that unanimity exists where it does not. For my part, I do not believe that a Christian is obligated, *de fide*, to be a pacifist. The logic of pacifism would deprive policemen of their guns and entrust the protection of life, limb, and property to moral suasion—a program that original sin would nullify. There have been wars in the past which probably resulted in more good than harm, such as the American War of Independence and the medieval revolt of the Swiss cantons. Other wars, such as the most recent one, led to no good, but prevented intolerable evil; the justification for fighting Hitler is not that Europe is in a wholesome condition today but that, if war had not been waged, the whole continent—perhaps the whole world—would be part of the Thousand Year Reich.

Having said this, I must raise a question which I shall not attempt to answer. The nature of war has changed so much that the word hardly means what it did as late as the eighteenth century. The indiscriminate slaughter of enemy civilians, the collapse of almost every vestige of military fair play, the inevitable starvation in the wake of war—these make it dubious whether the results of a future war can ever make up for the price exacted.

I do not believe the question is one involving absolute principles but a kind of Christianized common sense. As I have said, I shall not presume to give an answer. If the Christians of the future, confronted by the likelihood of war, should decide to have no part in it, they can at least experiment with one substitute which has proved successful against a relatively humane adversary. Whether it would work against completely fanatical and doctrinaire totalitarians, we have no way of knowing. I am thinking, of course, of Gandhi's use of nonviolence.

Satyagraha, as the Indians call it, is possible only when the masses of people are inwardly disciplined and willing to sacrifice their liberty and possibly their lives for a common cause. Its very renunciation of violence imposes a heavy strain on human nature. It was the achievement of Gandhi to instill into his followers some of his own qualities, so that they could meet the test. If *satyagraha* ever becomes necessary in the West, the religious leaders will face a similar responsibility.

It is possible, of course, that *satyagraha* will not take root in the West, and that wars—waged with today's weapons or worse—will break out. In that case, the nonpacifist Christian will have a peculiarly important mission: to fight without deep-seated hate, to keep alive in the very midst of war the possibility of future reconciliation, to combat every impulse in himself and others to regard the enemy as permanent and hopeless beasts. More soldiers than are generally realized succeeded in doing this during the last war. Many of them fought and fought well with no hatred in their hearts, and returned home shocked to find the implacable hatred of the enemy voiced by armchair sitters.

Most important of all, if wars come and Christians fight, they can exert a strong influence after the war to lessen the harshness of victory. To some extent this has been done after World War II. To give one example—*The Christian Century* was one of the few magazines that plainly denounced the savage Potsdam agreement when it was first revealed, and exposed both its immoral nature and its impracticality. The progressive modification of American policies in Germany is not due entirely to rivalry with Russia: sensitive public opinion in this and other countries has kept the official conscience on edge.

As a postscript I must echo something I said in the Foreword. Very likely this entire discussion of war will be obsolete and unnecessary in a few years. If the only two great powers fight it out with atoms and germs, one nation will win and rule the world for a long time to come, or both will be so smashed up that wars for several centuries will be hardly more serious than local skirmishes between rival slot-machine gangs. Or, if peace is preserved for another fifteen or twenty years there will be time enough for the men of good will—Christian or otherwise—to work for the only goal that offers real hope of lasting peace. And that goal, beyond any doubt, is the end of sovereign states and the creation of world government.

The Family

The percentage of American marriages ending in divorce was about six times greater at the end of World War II than at the end of the Civil War. However, an increase in the divorce rate means nothing by itself. Broadly speaking, there are three possible viewpoints. The first, which is publicly expressed only by a few courageous theorists but is widely held in private, is that of the person who regards progress as a grand game of shaking off taboos. To him the divorce figures mean that human liberty has advanced with great strides since 1865.

The second, and most vocal viewpoint is that of the "social and antisocial" school. The frequency of divorce is a bad thing not because it violates any law of God but because it produces confusion and breaks down the structure of society. The typical social scientist urges married couples to resort to the divorce court only in the most extreme cases. The difficulty here is that the argument of "social utility" is an abstract one to the man or woman enamored of the charming person who might be the next spouse; the obligation to society seems a pale thing beside the impulsions of personal longing.

The third viewpoint is the Christian one. Throughout most of Christian history the Church has stubbornly insisted that marriage is a lifelong relationship which can be ended (with privilege of remarriage) only in case of death. Some denominations include a few other grounds, usually adultery or permanent desertion. In any case, the position of the Church has been implacably opposed to the modern free-and-easy attitude toward divorce and remarriage, and to the equally casual practice that prevailed in Rome and Jerusalem at the time of Christ.

It is true that in recent years certain denominations have relaxed their marriage discipline, so that divorced couples can remarry and remain members of the Church. Such modification of the Church's stand has generally been justified by vague and rather sentimental talk about the spirit of Christ's teachings as opposed to the letter. The real motive has probably been to recognize a de facto situation which the Church felt powerless to oppose. Or, in some cases, the relaxation of discipline may have resulted from the pervasive secularization of the Church: a loss of its distinctive message in marriage as in almost everything else.

All this is water over the dam. In judging what the future attitude of the Church should be it is necessary first of all to ask, "What is the Christian concept of marriage?"

Several false ideas need to be cleared away. To begin with, Christianity is not against marriage. Even those denominations which encourage monasticism regard the latter as the vocation for a specialized few; marriage is the normal way of life for Christians. Christianity is also not against sex, not against the body and its functions. More than any other great religion, Christianity takes the physical world seriously and endeavors to glorify it by using it for spiritual ends. As evidence of this, we have the fact that the ideal of romantic love between husband and wife scarcely exists outside the Christian world, and most of the world's great love poetry has been written in Christian civilizations. Most emphatic of all, marriage has always been regarded by most Christians as one of the sacraments—"an outward and visible sign of an inward and spiritual grace."

Christ's teachings about marriage go back to a concept involving more than a casual mating, civil contract, or business partnership. They hark back, in fact, to the story of Adam and Eve which tells how Adam looked at the newly created Eve and said, "This is now bone of my bones, and flesh of my flesh: she shall be called Woman, because she was taken out of Man. Therefore shall a man leave his father and his mother, and shall cleave unto his wife: *and they shall be one flesh*" [italics mine].

When the Pharisees, vainly trying to trip Him up, asked Christ whether a man could divorce his wife, He replied by the quotation given above. They had a rejoinder ready: "Why did Moses then command to give a writing of divorcement, and to put her away?" To which Christ answered that Moses had merely made a realistic but temporary concession: "Moses because of the hardness of your heart suffered you to put away your wives: but from the beginning it was not so."

I suppose that many moderns—including some orthodox Christians—would not be unduly impressed by the marriage doctrines propounded by Adam, a person whose historicity is unproved and unprovable. However, by quoting the passage from Genesis, Christ affirmed the teaching summarized in it—that marriage is not merely a mechanical or legal union but so complete a merging of two lives that the husband and wife become "one flesh," one organism. Their sexual union is only part of the complete union, which is also psychological and spiritual. To separate the two partners of such a merging is rather like hacking the leg off one man and trying to graft it onto another man's thigh.

It is a stern, inexorable doctrine of marriage. The objections come quickly to mind. Had Christ never seen unhappy marriages? He assuredly had. He grew up in Nazareth, a turbulent caravan center. He had doubtless observed husbands beating their wives and wives shrieking curses at their husbands. His childhood was not a sheltered one.

Perhaps it was because of the very depth of His insight and the acuteness of His observation that He sanctioned few or no escape clauses. He never forgot that man is a fallen being—that original sin had erased the pretty picture of spontaneous goodness, and had left in every man and woman a wild restlessness and nagging selfishness. Christ came to teach not angels but men. It may be that He knew if one gave them an inch they would take an ell; that the realistic concessions of Moses were rapidly wrecking marriage as a permanent union.

This is all by way of commentary. The reader who regards it (perhaps rightly) as an impertinence is free to dismiss it. The plain teachings of Christ remain.

I have said that Christ based His attitude on the assumption that the husband and wife are an organism which cannot be hacked in two without intolerable damage. This way of putting it may sound too foreign to modern habits of thought. For a more detailed analysis I suggest one of the most profound sociological descriptions yet penned: the statement of purposes in the marriage service of the Church of England:

Holy Matrimony . . . is an honourable estate, instituted of God in the time of man's innocency, signifying unto us the mystical union that is betwixt Christ and his Church . . . and is commended of Saint Paul to be honourable among all men: and therefore is not by any to be enterprised, nor taken in hand, unadvisedly, lightly, or wantonly, to satisfy man's carnal lusts and appetites, like brute beasts that have no understanding; but reverently, discreetly, advisedly, soberly, and in the fear of God; duly considering the causes for which matrimony was ordained.

First, It was ordained for the procreation of children, to be brought up in the fear and nurture of the Lord, and to the praise of his Holy Name.

Secondly, It was ordained for a remedy against sin, and to avoid fornication; that such persons as have not the gift of continence might marry, and keep themselves undefiled members of Christ's body.

Thirdly, It was ordained for the mutual society, help and comfort, that the one ought to have of the other, both in prosperity and adversity. . . .

In these three clauses we have the historic Christian doctrine of marriage. At first glance, the reasons given (though candid enough) seem far removed from romantic love. But I should like to suggest that the picture painted is a much more inclusive one than the modern secular theory of marriage—that, in fact, it includes every valid aspect of the latter. Taking the clauses one at a time—

Matrimony was ordained for the procreation of children. To the husbands and wives of an earlier period, this must have sounded like a truism. Children, whether wanted or not, were the usual result of marriage. With the development and increasing efficiency of birth control, a larger element of free will is involved.

In the question of birth control, as in the matter of war, the Christian world speaks with a divided voice. The Roman Catholic Church is adamant in its insistence that mechanical or chemical contraception is a violation of "natural law," but it tolerates the so-called "rhythm method," which depends on the menstrual cycle. Most of the churches are noncommittal, and some, such as the Anglican Communion, have gone on record as approving birth control in certain circumstances. It is a complicated moral and practical question, and the varying viewpoints, while confusing, are not surprising.[1] I can only say that the all-out opponents of birth control seem to me to be overlooking one possibility: that birth control, by giving couples the power to decide between five, two, or no children, throws squarely upon them a basic moral choice. Perhaps God so guides history that moral freedom is constantly increased and the consequences of individual decisions become more momentous. Birth control, like atomic energy, can be used for good or evil purposes.

During the 1920's it was the fashion to seize upon contraception and use it to avoid children altogether, or at least severely limit the number of them. Today the doctrine of "children last" seems to be losing adherents rapidly. The no-child or one-child family is becoming almost a rarity, even in many professional circles. I doubt that the increased willingness to beget children springs in most cases from religious motives. A secularist with open eyes can learn the value of children simply by observing the life led by most childless couples.

I say *most* childless couples, for I am thinking exclusively of couples who refrain from having children because they prefer automobiles or the freedom to get about. Childless couples who are childless against their will—victims of physical conditions that make conception impossible or too dangerous to risk—are in an entirely different category. The bitter frustration in their lives is often transmuted into an

[1] The sanest discussion that I have come across is: Gilbert Russell, *Men and Women*, London: SCM Press Ltd., 1948). Unfortunately no American publisher has as yet brought out an edition of this excellent book.

outgoing love and helpfulness toward other people's children, so that in effect they become the foster parents of an immense family. Nor am I thinking of the occasional situations in which a husband and wife lead such unusual and hazardous lives—missionaries, explorers, experimenters in medical research—that they dare not subject children to the same risk. Such marriages, though childless, can be thoroughly sacramental in quality.

No, I am thinking of couples who can't be bothered. Many of them are drab sights when they reach middle age. The attempt to make the country club, the bridge party, or civic activities into satisfactory substitutes for children is seldom successful. The romantic glamour fades into a matter-of-fact fondness and familiarity; indeed, the glamour seems to vanish more swiftly and surely with childless couples than with those who throw themselves into the mutual business of child rearing. The lives of such couples become increasingly pointed toward the past, for they have no children to point them toward the future.

Occasionally one still meets couples who expound the philosophy of childlessness. They expatiate on the horrible state of the world (which is nothing new; it has always been dreadful) and state that they would not be so immoral as to hurl new lives into the atomic age. However, if the world is too cruel for children, it is also too cruel for adults, but one does not see many of these philosophers reaching for the convenient revolver. That they continue living suggests that most of them refrain from having children, not because they are kindhearted but because they fear children would get in the way.

So they would. Once the child arrives, he calmly becomes the center of the stage. Except in those rare families that can afford a maid, the mother devotes her days to taking care of the child, and the father is pressed into service at bathtime when he comes home from the factory or office. Mealtimes are not tranquil. If the parents are suddenly invited out for an evening's gaiety, they either locate a "sitter" or stay home. The new dress or overcoat must wait until Junior's tonsil operation is paid for.

Christianity does not pretend that you can get something for nothing; it does say that you can get very much for very little. It is true that children are expensive, time-consuming, patience-taxing additions to the family, but the sacrifices they demand are trivial compared to what they offer.

Every sensitive person is troubled by the question: "What can I do to make the world a little less of a mess than it is? I can vote for the best candidates, I can organize humanitarian movements, but what I accomplish seems so little compared to what remains to be done. What can I do specifically that no one else can do?" the answer is a terrifying challenge: Beget children, and do the best job you can rearing them.

In the family there can be no evading responsibility. The school, the Church itself can make only clumsy attempts to do what the family is designed to do. The child's total way of looking at the world is largely determined by how its parents behave and what attitude governs their lives. The parents can rear three or four children to add to the maladjustment and confusion of the world, or they can give the world three or four children who have sufficient stability and moral firmness to stand up to chaos without being engulfed by it.

The paradox in the whole situation is that the parents who forget their own wishes in solicitude for their children are rewarded out of all proportion to their deserts. It is a question whether the relation between husband and wife or that between parent and child is the closer. Certainly the two relationships are the closest that most human beings are ever likely to experience, short of the ideal relationship toward God. And the parent finds that the hours of tedious and often nerve-wracking attention he gives to his children end in something of such richness that he is tongue-tied when he tries to describe it to his childless friends.

The question of children or no children does not stand by itself. The real question is life-affirmation or life-negation. If the whole business of existence is a mistake, children are a part of the mistake: but if life, despite the corruptions that man constantly introduces into it, is essentially and gloriously good, then children are a passionate declaration of affirmation. To have them and rear them is to wave the red banner of revolt against all faintness of heart, all defeatism, all easy philosophies of *après moi le déluge.*

Matrimony was ordained for a remedy against sin, and to avoid fornication. This clause, often singled out as especially offensive, is merely realistic. The sexual instincts of man and the animals cannot really be compared. Most animals have definite mating seasons and can scarcely be aroused to sexual desire at other times of the year. Sex is a more constant tyrant with humans than with animals. It is so imperious that only the exceptional person dare undertake a life of virginity. It is unthinkable for most people. And, since from both a sociological and a religious point of view, promiscuity is the creator of social confusion and personal unhappiness, there seems nothing shameful about having an honorable "remedy against sin."

A series of temporary alliances might satisfy us if we were merely animals. But we cannot isolate sex from everything else in life. It entwines itself with lyric poetry, the painting of pictures, the composition of music, and the creation of philosophic systems. Like religion, it cuts across all boundary lines. For this reason, the casual animal solution leads not to fulfillment but to the psychiatrist.

The only solution that will satisfy the imperious instinct and at the same time avoid a sense of incompleteness is the permanent sexual union. Marriage makes it possible to relate sex to everything else. It becomes meaningful because of all the shared experiences—children, home, books, ideas, vacations, work, religion, gardening, even arguments up to a point.

Specialization is the curse of modern society; the carpenter, the bond salesman, and the professor are lonely because they don't know what to talk about when they meet. Sex, isolated à la Kinsey, injects the same poisonous specialization into human relationships; the frustrations and neuroses begin to flourish. Only when woven into the entire fabric of two lives does its full richness become possible. The other side of "a remedy against sin" is "the way to make sex really meaningful."

Matrimony was ordained for the mutual society, help and comfort, that the one ought to have of the other, both in prosperity and adversity. It is possible to love everybody, or almost everybody, in the Christian sense and still feel a gaping loneliness, a desire for a particularly close relationship with a handful of people or with one person.

Marriage is the best possibility for banishing this kind of loneliness. In a reasonably satisfactory marriage there may be blank spots—places where understanding breaks down—but fewer than are found in even a close friendship. And there is the blessed freedom from keeping up a front—the worst and the best are known, and shared.

Marriage is also a way of reducing the terrors of old age. Society may provide medical care and "homes" for the aged, but the gift is grudging and impersonal. The human need is for one person who cares completely and is willing quite matter-of-factly to stay with you "in prosperity and adversity." Marriage provides this opportunity, and in the completeness of the self-giving love of husband and wife, parents and children, it makes more understandable the sacrificial love of God Himself.

It may be asked where romantic love fits into all this. I think the term needs to be defined. Often it means no more than a strong rush of yearning, accompanied perhaps by dreamy idealization of the beloved. Such an emotion may lead to either a happy or an unhappy marriage, depending on all the other factors. If the marriage is successful, the first flush of feeling may change into a steadier, less volatile love, or it may acquire greater body without losing the pristine glamour.

But by romantic love one may also mean the experience of Dante with Beatrice. Charles Williams has given the classical analysis of it in *He Came Down from Heaven*, and I agree with him that the experience is a genuine revelation of what mankind was meant to be at Creation: the lover sees the beloved *sub specie aeternitatis*—as one might imagine Adam seeing all things, with the glory of Creation fresh upon them. Such a love may or may not result in marriage; when it does, the awareness may fade away or may linger. If it remains, one can only say that the marriage is blessed by an extra grace additional to the general sacramental grace of marriage.

The Christian doctrine of marriage is clear enough. What should the churches do about it? First of all, they should teach it. The teaching ought to have a double effect. Christ's emphasis on the permanence of marriage would discourage hasty rushing to the altar with the half-concealed thought,

"Well, if it doesn't work out, I can go to Nevada." The second—and more important result—should be to make people see *greater* possibilities in marriage. By lifting marriage from the shallowly sentimental or equally shallow pragmatic level on which it rests today, its unfolding possibilities would be revealed, with the consequence that, if only a half or a fourth of the possibilities were actually realized in a given marriage, the reward would still be so great that the minor dislocations that now lead to the divorce court would be seen as trivial blemishes.

The churches could be particularly helpful when couples come asking to be married. Many churches have a series of confirmation classes which prospective members must attend. The same need exists for instruction in marriage. It should be thorough, frank, and unapologetically Christian. The minister or priest would be wise to enlist the aid of Christian physicians and psychologists. After a man and his fiancée had been thus instructed, the church could marry them with a clearer conscience and greater hopes for their success.

But the distasteful word "discipline" cannot be evaded. During most of Christian history the churches have taken it for granted that part of their function was to enforce certain moral standards on their members. This does not mean that any Christian is ever free of sin; it merely means that becoming a Christian is rather like joining an army: the volunteer cannot expect all the comforts and easygoing ways of home. The churches can choose either to take the dictates of Christ seriously or they can continue their effort to work out a negotiated peace with the world.

I believe the latter attempt is futile from a pragmatic viewpoint. The world will not negotiate a compromise peace; it demands unconditional surrender. Very rightly.

the world's opinion of the churches sinks every time the churches make a gesture of appeasement. Often the greatest service the churches can render the world is to be stubborn. If the churches recover their vitality, I should expect one of the first indications to be a forthright determination to regain the right to hold their members up to the explicit demands of Christianity in regard to marriage.

Some theorists would contend that the churches should also insist on having the same standards embodied in the civil law. During the Middle Ages this was perhaps reasonable, since practically everyone was, at least nominally, a Christian. It is doubtful whether such uniformity will ever prevail again. I do not believe that Christians, even if in a majority, have the right to impose their peculiar teachings on everyone else. They should simply support the reforms now advocated by many secular authorities. These might include a uniform national marriage and divorce law, and the elimination of trivial grounds for divorce. Longer waiting periods before a divorce, the employment of experienced psychologists to effect reconciliations—these are among the promising suggestions frequently made by specialists. And, it goes almost without saying, the churches should preach the necessity of governmental action to assure adequate housing; overcrowding is in itself the principal factor in many broken marriages.

But laws really amount to very little unless the individual is sound. So here, as in many other cases, the problem comes back to the individual. And the greatest contribution that Christianity and the churches can make is not so much to repeat endlessly the grim "thou shalt not's" of the Christian doctrine of marriage (though they should be repeated occasionally), as to awake the individual to as full an awareness as possible of what Christianity is, and in particular to make him see the uniquely rewarding nature of Christian marriage—the way that it answers so many seemingly unrelated human needs. A wit once said of God that if He did not exist, man would have to invent Him. The same thing is true of marriage and the family. The point where Christianity takes leave of secular thinking about marriage is there. Christianity says that man did not have to; God was the inventor.

10

Education

The first thing that strikes many foreigners studying American education is its dualism. The elementary and high schools concern themselves with many interesting things; they do not shy away from controversial matters like politics and racial relations; they have time for an increasing variety of vocational subjects—on only one matter of universal concern are they silent: religion.

The reason is, of course, the separation of Church and State—a principle embodied in the First Amendment to the federal Constitution, and designed to prevent an entangling alliance between sectarian factions and the government. By legal decisions and still more by the evolution of public attitudes toward it, the amendment has expanded in scope until it seems to impose a vast conspiracy of silence on the public schools. Only the marginal aspects of religion can be taught without danger of a writ of mandamus. In so far as religion figures in the curriculum at all it weaves in and out of medieval history like European cathedrals and suits of mail.

This has important consequences. The child spends twenty-five or thirty hours a week in school, learning many valuable and enthralling things, but religion is not one of them. After school hours he is still under the influence of the school—his Boy Scout troop is sponsored by the school, and so is his athletic team or his theatrical group. Most of his waking time is spent in school, preparing for school, or taking part in school-sponsored activities. Quite logically he concludes that what he does most of the time must be very important, and other possible interests are of less value.

On Sunday the Church makes a desperate attempt to seize the typical school child and cram him full of a week's dose of religious instruction in one hour's time. Capturing him is the first problem; no truant officer disturbs the repose of the parents if they choose to slumber till eleven. Once captured, the child is seldom impressed with the room in which he learns of the Maker of Heaven and Earth. An occasional wealthy church may have classrooms and teaching equipment equal to that of the public schools; the average church is not so fortunate. The Sunday-School room is generally a catchall. Choir members, arriving late, swish their robes against the pupils as they hurry past. Classes of different age groups fidget at tables in the four corners of the room. By one window the three-to-five's are coloring pictures; at the other window are the six-to-nine's, spelling their way through the story of the good Samaritan. In another corner of the chaos ten-to-twelve's are audibly learning a catechism. If the heroic teachers maintain sufficient order to protect the minister's sermon from distant outcries, they are judged successful.

The child, not unreasonably, concludes that what he learns in one confused hour a week is unimportant in comparison with the instruction he receives twenty-five or thirty hours a week in incomparably better surroundings. The whole situation has become so disastrous that for the past couple of decades experiments have been made in many communities to find a way of relating religious and secular education, so as to put an end to the dualism. The problem is also receiving study by interfaith groups; one of them, which has been at work since 1944, recently published its report,[1] to which I am indebted for several of the ideas advanced in this chapter.

Can any general principles be suggested? To avoid over-optimism I shall assume that for a long time to come we shall still be beset with many and competitive denominations. Bearing this in mind, I suggest that there are at least four basic principles:

1. Since Christians believe that their religion is the most important thing in their own lives, they are both morally and psychologically obligated to see that their children learn it in all its fullness.

2. If Christianity is going to be learned it must be taught by someone, and taught in such a way that its importance is obvious. In an age of catacombs, the secrecy and danger connected with religious instruction suffice to make clear its importance, but in an atmosphere of neutrality it is essential that Christianity be imparted in surroundings as impressive as those associated with football tactics, home economics, and algebra.

3. Ideally, the family should provide much more religious instruction than it usually does, but the family could never be a complete solution. Not all parents are expert teachers, and there are too many distractions in family life. The greatest Christian influence that parents can have on their children is indirect.

4. In the past, many Christian denominations have used

[1] *The Relation of Religion to Public Education: The Basic Principles,* The Committee on Religion and Education of the American Council on Education, 744 Jackson Place, Washington 6. Reprinted in the May-June, 1947, issue of *Religious Education.* Anyone interested in the problem should by all means read the report, which shows every indication of careful research and creative thought. For a general critique of American education on all levels, I strongly recommend B. I. Bell's trenchant book, *Education in Crisis* (New York: Whittlesey House, 1949).

strong-arm methods to force their faith down the throats of the reluctant. This is plainly repugnant to the spirit of Christ. Any educational system that incorporates Christianity must lean over backward to respect the rights and sensibilities of non-Christian religious groups, agnostics, and atheists.

One attempted solution that seems at first glance to meet all these requirements is "released time." Its details vary from community to community, but the typical arrangement provides that any child, whose parents so request, may be excused from regular classes for a certain length of time each week in order to receive instruction from the minister of his church or some other person selected for the purpose. The classes in religion have sometimes been held in public school buildings; in other communities, churches and parish houses have been used.

According to various estimates, between two and three thousand communities had such systems in operation when the matter came up before the federal Supreme Court in the now famous case of *McCollum* v. *Champaign*.[2] The Court, by its 8-to-1 decision, has thrown the whole situation into such confusion that no one knows whether all released-time systems are unconstitutional or only the particular kind in use at Champaign, Illinois. Some commentators hold that the Champaign system was ruled out mainly because the classes in religion were held in the public school buildings, and the attendance machinery of the schools was employed to see that children who had signed up for instruction actually appeared. Only a series of test cases from other cities can determine whether the Supreme Court will permit a sys-

[2] A copy of the decision may be obtained for twenty cents from the United States Government Printing Office, Division of Public Documents, Washington 25.

tem of released time if the classes are conducted in church buildings and the school merely dismisses the pupils without trying to check up on their attendance.

Assuming, however, that ways can be found of reconciling the First Amendment and released time, there are still serious objections to the system. For one thing, it accentuates sectarianism, according to many of its critics. In all their other studies the pupils meet together under the same teachers. Only when the children are to be taught religion are they sent off in different directions, to learn in one place that man is saved by faith, in another that he is saved by good works; to be told in one place that the pope is the vicar of Christ, and in another that he is the antichrist.

This criticism poses a problem which has been met by the Protestant churches in some communities through concerted action. They have worked out a uniform syllabus and pooled their teachers. This, of course, does not completely eliminate sectarianism—the Roman Catholics and Jews necessarily remain apart from such an arrangement—but it greatly reduces it and produces more religious unity than exists on the adult, churchgoing level.

However, even if the churches fail to co-operate in some communities, the charge of sectarianism cannot be regarded as a complete condemnation of released time, unless the critic is willing to go all the way and demand that the denominations should either be abolished by national ukase or forcefully merged.

A more serious objection to released time is that it does not really integrate secular and religious instruction. The Supreme Court decision makes it clear that the classes—if they are legal at all—cannot be held on school property; the teachers are different; the atmosphere of something "extra" hovers about the instruction. The system is better than Sunday school, but the dualism remains.

To end the dualism, the only solution is to devise a way to include religious studies in the standard curriculum of the public schools and to have the usual teachers conduct the courses. Such courses would be intended solely to give objective information, not to convert. Since a program of this sort would not require the participation of the churches in its administration, the Supreme Court might be willing to affix its *nihil obstat.*

I think I see how some of the details could be worked out, with fairness to all religious and antireligious viewpoints. For example, modern schools generally emphasize "social studies" a great deal. The pupils are taught about banks, labor unions, supply and demand, welfare organizations, the political structure of the country. Since it cannot be disputed that the churches and synagogues are among the oldest and most influential social institutions, they could be studied along with the other organizations. This would not have much to do with the intricacies of theology, but it would help to destroy the feeling that religious institutions are in a pariah category unfit to be mentioned in class. Information concerning them could easily be worked into revised editions of existing textbooks.

The Bible needs to be studied for several reasons. In the first place, English and American literature is almost a closed book without a background in the Judaeo-Christian tradition. For example, I challenge anyone to teach seventeenth-century poetry without spending a third of his time explaining the Biblical allusions. Also (as is stated so frequently that it seems a truism) the Bible is one of the monuments of English literature in its own right, and its style echoes in writers as diverse as Abraham Lincoln and Walt

Whitman. Furthermore, the social ideas contained in the Bible have had so far-reaching an influence that it is impossible to understand half the proposals made by modern agnostic reformers without a familiarity with the Bible.

I do not think it greatly matters whether the Bible is studied as a separate course, or whether it is worked into other courses wherever relevant. The essential thing is to give the child a general familiarity with it, for otherwise his education is peripheral.

The Talmud should also be studied, regardless of whether any Jewish children are in the particular school. The Talmud's close kinship with the Bible and the large part the Jews have played in creating our common civilization are reason enough. Some study of the Talmud would also help dispel the bizarre notions that occasional Christians still have about Judaism. Christian children would benefit from its study, just as Jewish children reading the New Testament would benefit. In neither case would there be any question of conscience, for no pupil would be asked to accept the religion he was studying.

This choice of religious classics may seem provincial. Why not include the Koran, the Bhagavad-Gita, and the Analects of Confucius? Ideally, one should. But there is not time for everything. The Bible and the Talmud are most essential for the American school child simply because our culture is Judaeo-Christian in origin.

Acquaintance with the Bible and the Talmud, and some introduction to the churches and the synagogues as social institutions would do a great deal to end the dualism. However, one thing more should be done. The pupils need to learn what Judaism and Christianity *are*.

Here the cry of sectarianism is sure to be raised, but it is a false cry. The courses can be worked out in such a way that they are not slanted in favor of any particular religion or denomination. The purpose of them would be not to evangelize but to inform. A more realistic objection concerns the difficulty of finding teachers with enough objectivity to teach such courses without slanting their presentation to favor one sect at the expense of the others. It *would* require a high degree of integrity, but the same thing is true of civics. What good New Dealer but feels his heart beat faster when he describes the F.D.R. era? What Republican of the old school, whose face does not twitch with anger when he mentions the T.V.A.? But civics is still taught in the schools without too much public tumult. If Congregationalists are afraid of having their children taught a course in religion by a Presbyterian, a Republican ought to be equally afraid of having his child study civics, or almost anything else, under a Democrat.

If such a program were attempted, it might begin in the freshman year of high school. Each pupil would then take a one-semester course in Judaism. The textbook would be written by outstanding Jewish and Christian scholars and its purpose would be twofold: to show the development and present form of Judaism, and to give the historical background of Christianity.

During the second semester the pupil would take a course in basic Christian theology and morality. The most useful definition of "basic Christian theology" for it has been the point of departure for nearly all later developments—would be the statements of belief formulated at Nicaea and the other "general councils" of the Church during the first five or six centuries. A study of these doctrinal statements, supplemented by reading large portions of the New Testament, would give the pupils a clear picture of classical Christian theology—which incidentally is considerably easier to understand than alegbra or the niceties of English grammar. They would be free to accept it, wholly or in part, or reject it in toto. Their grades would depend on knowing it, not on believing in it. Coupled with the study of theology, would be a simple examination of Christian morality, as set forth in the New Testament.

From the religious viewpoint, the great thing gained from such a course would be that the pupils who had taken it would never toss over their religion out of sheer ignorance. Most of the college students who become atheists after studying biology or anthropology do so because their ten-year-old variety of religion cannot stand up against adult science.

In the second year of high school there might well be a required course in "types of Christianity." This would serve two purposes: to teach the pupil more about his own church, and, if possible, to give him increased respect for other denominations. In America such a course could begin with the Roman Catholic Church and the closely related Eastern Orthodox Church, go on to the Anglican Communion, and then take up the major families of Protestant churches: Lutheran, Calvinistic, Baptist, etc.

Two years would probably be enough to require. For pupils who wanted to explore the religious traditions of other civilizations a third course might be offered in comparative religion.

A system of religious instruction such as that just outlined, supplemented by a certain amount of released time (the Supreme Court willing) for more detailed study under the direct control of the churches, might possibly be sufficient to end religious illiteracy and eliminate the dangerous dualism of public education. If such a program were put into effect, the Sunday school could be converted into an hour for worship—a children's service, to prepare them for the regular service.

I can see nothing in the program that should trouble the most conscientious atheist, for at no stage of schooling would his child be asked to *believe* the things he studied. However, the individual must be the final judge of his own conscience. If atheists or agnostics felt that they could not send their children to public schools of this sort, they should be free to establish their own schools, subsidized from public funds.

The sword of the Supreme Court hangs over even this moderate program. If the program should be attempted and encounter the veto of the Supreme Court, only two recourses would be left. The first, which would be difficult but not impossible, would be to amend the federal Constitution by making the First Amendment considerably more explicit than it is at present. The outlawing of a state church, the principle of neutrality as between competing sects—these are vital and should remain. But it should not be past the ingenuity and common sense of legislators to spell out in detail the particular kinds of religious instruction that can be integrated with secular instruction without breaking down the necessary wall between Church and State.

The second alternative—if the Supreme Court imposes its veto on every attempted solution, and the First Amendment remains unchanged—is for the churches to set up schools of their own and teach the three R's and all other secular subjects in addition to the fourth R.

If the churches once decide that the chances of integrating religious and secular instruction in the public schools are hopeless, and that the only solution is a system of church schools—that is the end of the public schools. After the children of church members are withdrawn and placed in church schools, there will be no incentive for Christians to vote huge sums of money to maintain schools that are of no benefit to them.

I hope that I have not pictured the public schools as evil institutions, staffed by scheming men and women intent on destroying the religious faith of the younger generation. There are no personal villains, no incarnate devils in the situation. I should suspect that schoolteachers, as a class, tend to be more devout than the statistically average American. It is the setup as a whole that exercises a steady and almost irresistible pressure. Year by year religion is pushed into a smaller corner of the child's life. He simply hasn't enough time for it, and it seems peripheral to his major activities.

Almost everyone would prefer to see the problem solved without the destruction of the public school system. Americans are justly proud of their tax-supported education. It breaks down social barriers; it prepares students for civic life; it is manned, on the whole, by intelligent and self-sacrificing teachers and administrators. The problems created by its destruction would be very serious. A town of four thousand might have a dozen church schools: Roman Catholic, Lutheran, Episcopalian, Baptist, Methodist, Four Square Gospel, Congregational, and all the rest. The facilities would be wretched in most cases, the teachers poorly prepared, the atmosphere inbred.

If worst did come to worst, the situation could be eased a great deal by co-operative ventures between churches with approximately the same doctrines. For example, the Lutherans and Episcopalians might jointly establish a school, and pledge themselves to keep silent on the apostolic succession and a few other touchy points.

The utopian solution, as I see it, is the integration of religious and secular instruction in the public schools. However, a certain number of church schools in all the denominations would be very desirable. Being privately controlled, they can experiment more freely; their independence also lessens the danger that a whole generation of conformists will be turned out by the public schools. One of their most valuable functions could be to train a Christian cadre: to give their pupils a particularly rich grounding in Christianity and its implications. The teacher in a church school has freedom to show the relevance of religion to everything else. The textbooks could be written from a candidly religious viewpoint. For example, a text on astronomy would perhaps point out that the vast distances of space and the marvelous intricacy of the stellar system are reflections of the majesty and creativeness of God; a biology manual could relate the process of evolution to the will of God; a sociology book would not be content to *describe* society: it would also inquire how far particular social institutions are in harmony with Christianity. The list could be extended endlessly. The result, in such church schools, should be that the pupils would acquire the conviction that their faith is relevant to everything.

Almost everything said so far has concerned the pupil and his curriculum. Regardless of what system or systems evolve, the teacher would respond to the impact of an awakened Christianity. Teaching cannot be effectively done in a vacuum or in chaos; the Christian lives in neither, and his inner security would be reflected in the quality and dedication of his teaching, and his increased understanding of the pupils.

I see now that this chapter is as lopsided as the one on the family. The problem of restoring religion to education looms so large that I have said scarcely a word about the broader effects on education of a revival of Christianity.

Several reforms should come about from the deadly seriousness with which Christianity regards the individual. Great progress has been made in the past century toward increasing educational opportunities and giving the child from poverty-stricken families a chance to get the best possible education, but a kind of sectional discrimination still exists. Some parts of the country have very limited tax resources, and these are the very sections where large families are the rule. The average Southern state, for example, spends a much higher percentage of its tax revenue on public education than does prosperous Pennsylvania or Ohio, but the funds made available are still pitifully inadequate, and the children spottily educated. The most elementary considerations of justice for the individual child would require taxing the wealthier regions to level up the standards of education throughout the country.

The Christian reverence for the individual would also do away with the more extreme features of so-called "progressive education." This system or philosophy of instruction has mutated into such varied forms since it was popularized by Professor John Dewey that it is difficult to describe it briefly. In its more bizarre manifestations, it seems to hold to the theory that if you let children do and study what they want to, they will swiftly recapitulate the history of the race, discover for themselves the principles of Euclid, learn to read by by-passing the alphabet, and emerge as well-educated adults without ever doing anything that wasn't just plain fun.

Children are intelligent. They see the nonsense in this. They know that they are not capable of deciding at the age of eleven what they will wish they had learned when they reach the age of twenty-one, and they wonder what adults are for, if not to guide them.

In actual practice, "progressive education" compromises with reality by subtly manipulating the pupils into thinking they want to learn useful facts and skills. The children are also aware of the manipulation. The teacher walks into the classroom, a book under one arm and a sheaf of theme paper under the other. He proceeds to read a story aloud, and the pupils whisper to one another, "He's going to make us want to write a theme about the story."

It is noteworthy that men and women educated in the more austere schools of times gone by seemed to specialize in vivid and forthright personalities; it is the graduates of the modern play-school systems of education who are so drearily standardized that they seem interchangeable. In a Christian society, the teacher would show his respect for the child by teaching him what he needed to know in order to grow up into genuine adulthood.

The Christian respect for the individual would improve the status of the very dull child. Everything possible would be done to aid him, but no longer would he be automatically promoted at the end of each year, and automatically given a diploma, identical with all other diplomas, at the end of twelve years. (I have been told there are schools where this is done.) It is almost impossible to deceive a child; he will detect the contempt and condescension if bad work is called good work. It is a much greater tribute to his dignity as a child of God either to flunk him or to put him in special classes where the work will be adapted to his capacities. His stupidity is nothing shameful; he should no more feel apologetic for it than a cripple should make excuses for not playing football. In this case, he should receive at graduation a diploma on a different color of sheepskin or in a different style of lettering, to distinguish his attainments from those of the more gifted students.

Nothing I can say will keep some readers from hurling the charge of "antidemocratic" at these suggestions. It depends on what you mean by the term. If educational democracy involves the belief that all people have the same intelligence and can profit by identical schooling, then the charge is justified. It seems obvious that there is a natural hierarchy of intelligence. It has nothing to do with economic status or family background. The son of a rich man may be fit only for the retarded class; a tenant farmer's daughter may be good material for a Ph.D. degree. Educational democracy—as I use the term—means equality of opportunity. Every child, no matter how poverty-stricken his family, should have the opportunity to continue his education until he comes to the limit of his capacities. The result would be that the natural hierarchy would become all the more noticeable, but there would be surprises—social lines would be cut across.

The Christian respect for the individual would also improve the status of the very bright child, who is now the forgotten man in most schools. He should never be made to feel apologetic for his I.Q., and he is less likely to become smug about it if he is given enough tough work to challenge his brains. As he progresses into high school he ought to be encouraged to study Latin, Greek, advanced algebra, physics, or anything else his mind can grapple with. No one should hint that it is undemocratic of him to be bright. And, both for his own sake and the sake of society which never has a surplus of brilliant minds, he should be enabled by large fellowships to continue his education.

The whole point I am really trying to make is that a Christian civilization would take both education and the individual much more seriously than today. It would mean business. I can foresee one desirable result. With students of reasonable intelligence, it should be possible to provide a thorough enough general education in high school so that those who went on to college could begin a broad specialization in their freshman year, and not be obliged to spend two years learning the things they should have been taught in high school.

I have in mind a high-school program that would be equally useful to the student who went on to college and to the one who did not. Perhaps the latter would need it most of all, because he would not have the future opportunities to fill in the gaps. Once a pupil has learned the educational "tools" (reading, writing, languages, mathematics, etc.)— and presumably he should have mastered most of them in elementary school—he should be ready in high school to study the basic things he will need to know in order to be fully human, whether he becomes a ditchdigger or a business executive.

I suggest that these basic things involve the understanding of one's relationship to (1) God, (2) oneself, (3) other people, and (4) the physical universe.

To achieve these four objectives, theology and philosophy are indispensable. History should also come into its own— but it would be history freed of the dogmatic assumptions of economic determinism, and broadened to show the development and interaction of ideas as well as impersonal social forces. Professor Arnold J. Toynbee's book, *A Study of History*, is an excellent example of what I mean. History is invaluable for revealing human nature in action. Literature and the arts, in their very different way, serve the same purpose.

The sciences would be studied not as rigidly separated

pigeonholes of knowledge, but for the total understanding they give of the material world, man's place in it, and for their relationship to theology, philosophy, and history. Finally, I should not be surprised to see a broadened and deepened combination of sociology and psychology develop—certainly the superficiality of such courses as taught today would not be tolerated—and largely take over the territory now covered by the various "social sciences."

As the reader can see, these few highly tentative guesses as to the direction in which education might evolve have a great deal in common with the suggestions of the modern humanists. But it is a humanism plus. Humanism by itself is constantly in danger of degenerating into dilettantism, shallow humanitarianism, strong-arm do-good-ism, or apathy. Humanism, Christianized, will be capable of moving forward. It will know where it is going, and have the power to go.

⁓ 11 ⁓

The Arts

Two contradictory theories have been widely held about the relationship between religion and the arts. The first is that the artist and the priest are of necessity mortal enemies; art expresses the glories of the world as it appears to un-regenerate eyes, while religion disregards the present world in its preoccupation with the world to come. When such a viewpoint prevails, the painter, musician, and poet tend to give the Church a wide berth, and the Church for its part systematically eliminates all traces of artistic intrusion from its worship. During the grimmest period of the Puritan movement, church edifices were built as austere as barns, and psalms were sung without benefit of instrumental accompaniment.

The opposite theory is that art and religion are pretty much the same thing. Matthew Arnold was probably responsible for the popularity of this comfortable doctrine. He elevated the artist into a priest, and encouraged the solemn hush that is often observed at art galleries and concerts. The Church, in self-defense, began to talk of worship as "the greatest art."

I believe that both of these theories are too simple to be true. The thing that art and religion have in common is that they are creative. But the artist and the saint are two dif-

154

ferent people. The saint creates by working on himself: he is his own block of marble. Or, to put it with more theological accuracy, he lets God work on and in him, until he becomes in some degree a living revelation of God's attributes.

The artist does not work on himself: he works on canvas or marble or sounds or words. He may, and often does, reveal the glory and attributes of God, but not in his life. He is the transmission belt. What he creates acquires autonomy, and exists outside himself. An occasional artist is also a saint, but the combination is coincidental. If the artist happens to be also a Christian, his salvation is not achieved through his art but through the means that are open to every believer.

With this essential distinction in mind—that art and religion are partly parallel but not identical—it is possible to speculate with some plausibility on the impact that a rebirth of Christianity might have on the arts.

Christianity would come as a liberator. It would liberate by banishing the horror of the commonplace. To Christianity nothing *is* commonplace. Everything, from the workings of the capillary system to the revolutions of the planets has an aura of the miraculous about it, because the mark of the Manufacturer is stamped on each tiniest part.

The mystics are often regarded as madmen simply because they take this truth for granted. The victim of the commonplace cannot see the high sanity in St. Francis' conversations with the birds, nor has he any more profound comment than "drivel" when other mystics, in halting language, try to tell how the very stones and trees by the roadside glow with supernatural light. The artist often perceives this radiance in his own way and expresses it without completely understanding it; he would perceive it more readily if he had a theology adequate to it.

The horror of the commonplace has been one of the main reasons for preoccupation with the perverted and the unpleasant in much of recent art. It has become almost an esthetic convention that the normal is unworthy of attention. Christianity, by destroying the commonplace, removes the necessity of venturing desperately into the jungles of the strange and abnormal. A novelist would be able to write about workaday people, for they would no longer be workaday in his eyes; painters would find that a Frank Lloyd Wright house can be as rewarding to set down on canvas as a shanty in the blighted areas.

Not that art in a Christian society would be all sweetness and light. The neurotic depths, the cruelty, the stupidity, the sordidness are real—they, too, are a part of human life, and fit material for the artist. Christianity has its hell as well as its heaven; its "Inferno" beside its *Golden Legend*. The new liberty of the artist would simply mean that he was free to deal with anything.

Closely connected with the banishment of the commonplace is the enlarged understanding of human nature that Christianity imparts. For over a century partial systems of psychology have had their day, one after the other. During the nineteenth century the Rousseauistic heresy of innate goodness was perhaps the favorite. Today various kinds of determinism picture man as a walking machine. And there are not lacking thinkers of a grimmer school who say that human nature is nothing but a black compound of selfishness and cruelty.

One reason for the unpopularity of Christianity is that it can never completely agree with any of the psychological theories which rise and fall with such regularity. To the

Rousseauist it says, "What about original sin?" To the determinist it says, "What about free will?" To the complete pessimist it points out the original goodness of man at Creation, and the survival of traces of that goodness and instinctive yearning for it.

Christian psychology is subtle because human nature is not simple. Christianity asserts that man is an animal, but more than an animal; that when he tries to be merely an animal he becomes something less and worse than an animal, and that when he is willing to be human he ends by becoming more than merely human. It insists that man is both body and soul, and that to disparage the body or to disparage the soul is equally heretical.

The importance of this for the artist is clear. It extends the sweep of art in two directions—up and down. The evil depicted in Dante's "Inferno" cannot be matched by the explorations of psychoanalysis; the beatitude of the "Paradiso" makes the ideal of the "well-adjusted personality" ring hollow.

The arts, therefore, should acquire from Christianity new breadth (thanks to the banishment of the commonplace) and new height and depth. Nothing need be lost. All the hard-fought-for liberties won during the past hundred years will fit within the framework of the larger liberty created by Christian psychology.

However, artists need more than liberty. They need a common set of symbols, a "frame of reference." Until recently they had it. In the eighteenth century it could be safely assumed that an educated man was familiar with the Bible and the main doctrines of Christianity, had read extensively in the Greek and Roman classics, and had a good deal of knowledge (though of a condescending kind) in regard to fairy tales and folklore. The less educated man might not know his Horace and Plutarch but he knew his Bible—at least secondhand, from hearing it preached—and his acquaintance with folklore excelled that of the gentleman.

The modern writer—to single out one kind of artist—cannot assume that his readers have any great store of knowledge in common, beyond the brute facts of biology and casual familiarity with the latest newspaper headlines. Urbanization has almost dried up folklore; the Latin and Greek classics have faded still further into limbo; the Bible is constantly praised but less constantly read.

In Russia the problem has been solved by using the writings of Marx, Lenin, and the other Communist scriptures as a frame of reference. In America, the closest approach to a frame of reference is the comic strips. However, it is difficult to express a profound view of life with symbols taken from "Little Orphan Annie" or even "Barnaby."

Whether classical learning and folklore will ever revive we have no way of knowing, but a revival of Christianity would at least make the general public familiar with the Bible, sacraments, theology, and historical figures of the faith. These would provide a minimum frame of reference.

Everything I have so far said has been concerned with the indirect impact of Christianity. I have not implied that every Christian sculptor would feel duty-bound to carve nothing but holy statues, and fiction would consist wholly of didactic novels. Christian art will come about when Christian artists write, compose, carve, and paint anything they want to. Some of it will also be produced by atheists unconsciously responding to the unspoken assumptions of a Christian age.

However, something should perhaps be said about the role of the Church as a patron of the arts. In past epochs this was of great importance and beneficial to both parties.

The Church, if it ponders the implications of the Incarnation and realizes that the material and the spiritual were married without need or possibility of divorce when Christ was born, will make the fullest possible appeal to the five senses in order to reach the sixth. The one thing essential is for church leaders, when they begin to enlist the aid of artists, to realize that it is not the year 1200.

A good rule of thumb by which to judge the religious vitality of a period is the architecture of its churches. The more the church buildings resemble models in a museum, the more the religion is a museum piece. As long as Christianity kept its buoyancy and life, church architecture evolved along with secular architecture. It is highly probable that many romantic, stained-glass-loving Christians of today would be shocked if they could be transported a hundred years into the future. The Christians of that time may have a high regard for St. Thomas Aquinas, but I doubt that they will imitate the architecture of his day. Instead of hiring mediocre architects to turn out pseudomedieval structures, they will seek out the Frank Lloyd Wrights and have them build churches genuinely functional and as modern in spirit as secular architecture. Then it will be obvious to the casual spectator that religion has emerged from the museum.

Church music has not fared quite as badly as architecture. The average hymnal is at least broad-minded; it includes selections ranging from the earliest hymns to the works of Homer Rodeheaver. However, it shies away from the really modern. In the melodies the influence of Debussy and Schönberg has scarcely been felt. As for the lyrics, even though they may have been composed only five years ago they almost invariably echo the diction and clichés of the past. Meanwhile a fair amount of religious poetry of high

quality is being written by really modern poets and is waiting to be set to music and put into the hymnals. I hope
someday to hear a church choir—or better yet, the entire
congregation—singing something like Gerard Manley
Hopkins' magnificent "Pied Beauty":[1]

> Glory be to God for dappled things—
>> For skies of couple-colour as a brinded cow;
>>> For rose-moles all in stipple upon trout that swim;
> Fresh-firecoal chestnut-falls; finches' wings;
>> Landscape plotted and pieced—fold, fallow, and plow;
>>> And áll trádes, their gear and tackle and trim.
>
> All things counter, original, spare, strange;
>> Whatever is fickle, freckled (who knows how?)
>> With swift, slow; sweet, sour; adazzle, dim;
> He fathers-forth whose beauty is past change:
>> Praise Him.

Modern religious painting and sculpture are in a very
depressing state. They reflect the backward look. At best
they represent gallant attempts to imitate the high points
of the past. At their worst, they are found in the covers
of Sunday-school leaflets and in the statuary of many Roman
Catholic churches.

If stained-glass windows are still in vogue a hundred years
from now, one might hope to see originality permitted and
encouraged. Saints need not have that long-necked Byzantine look; backgrounds need not be confined to the land-
scapes of early agrarian and pastoral societies. Some courageous innovator might, for example, create a stained-glass
window showing that outstanding modern Christian, Dr.
Albert Schweitzer, performing a surgical operation on a

---

[1] *Poems of Gerald Manley Hopkins* (3rd ed.; New York & London:
Oxford University Press, 1948), p. 74. Quoted by permission of the
publishers and the poet's family.

Negro at Lambaréné, or one depicting the celebration of the Mass amid the drill presses in a factory. Such startling uses of a traditional medium would dramatize the relevance of Christianity to all times and situations.

It is to the shame of the churches that they have done almost nothing with murals. The much-maligned federal art projects during the depression turned out dozens of murals (many excellent in quality) on secular subjects, and the post offices of many communities are the more interesting for them. Mural painting is one of the most vigorous arts in America, and many artists would leap at an opportunity to practice it in the service of the Church.

There is one particular aspect of religious art that should be briefly mentioned. During its periods of greatest vitality it has been brazenly anachronistic. The medieval artists dressed Christ and His disciples like medieval men and painted medieval castles in the background. The development of the historical sense in religious art seems to coincide with the feeling that Christianity is a period piece. The more carefully we clothe Christ in the garments of the first century, the more surely we will exclude Him from the twentieth or twenty-first century.

At least one modern artist has made exciting experiments in anachronism. Miss Lauren Ford, who lives on a farm near Bethlehem, Connecticut, paints scenes from the life of Christ against a New England background. For example, "Epiphany at Bethlehem, Connecticut," shows Mary, Joseph, and Jesus at the door of a New England barn; through the deep snow of the village the Wise Men and their camels make their way while the villagers, dressed in modern clothes, look on in amazement. It is difficult to describe the peculiar simplicity and reverence of this, and many other, canvases of Miss Ford.

Of all the arts that might be stimulated by the Church,

the drama has perhaps the richest potentialities. Everyone knows the close alliance between stage and Church during the Middle Ages, and the essential part that religious plays had in the life of the people. The connection gradually broke down until stage and pulpit were frequently at war with each other. In recent years organized attempts in America and England have endeavored to awaken church people to the value of religious drama and to turn their glance forward rather than backward. The most spectacular success has been achieved by the annual Festival of the Arts, sponsored by the Bishop of Chichester and held at Canterbury Cathedral. A series of notable modern religious plays has been successfully produced, including one which was later given in leading American theaters: T. S. Eliot's *Murder in the Cathedral*.

The play is interesting for several reasons, apart from the literary stature of its author. The language is a skillful combination of prose, free verse, and rhyme. The chorus is used effectively and without seeming a stale echo of the Hellenic past. The four Tempters are adapted from the abstractions of the medieval morality plays but the spirit in which they are employed is modern. The psychology of the play makes full use of modern insights. The total result is that the questions raised by the life and death of St. Thomas à Becket are made relevant to today.

Less actable but more interesting in certain ways is W. H. Auden's Christmas Oratorio, *For the Time Being*. Here a very illuminating use is made of anachronism. Near the beginning the Narrator links the first and twentieth centuries:[2]

[2] W. H. Auden, *For the Time Being* (New York: Random House, 1944). Quoted by permission of the publishers.

If, on account of the political situation,
There are quite a number of homes without roofs, and men
Lying about in the countryside neither drunk nor asleep,
If all sailings have been cancelled till further notice, . . .

The play has passages of deep insight. For example, in the
scene, "The Temptation of St. Joseph," Joseph complains
of feeling the eyes of the curious constantly on him, and
senses that people are whispering behind his back. In
despair he asks God the Father what he has done to merit
this torment, and Gabriel comes to answer him:

JOSEPH
How then am I to know,
Father, that you are just?
Give me one reason.

GABRIEL
No.

JOSEPH
All I ask is one
Important and elegant proof
That what my Love had done
Was really at your will
And that your will is Love.

GABRIEL
No, you must believe;
Be silent, and sit still.

The Narrator then appears and explains to Joseph that he
must make amends for all the slights and contempt that
men have visited upon women. The first two stanzas of his
rather long speech are:

For the perpetual excuse
Of Adam for his fall—"My little Eve,

God bless her, did beguile me and I ate,"
   For his insistence on a nurse,
All service, breast, and lap, for giving Fate
Feminine gender to make girls believe
That they can save him, you must now atone,
   Joseph, in silence and alone;
While she who loves you makes you shake with fright,
Your love for her must tuck you up and kiss good night.

   For likening Love to war, for all
The pay-off lines of limericks in which
The weak resentful bar-fly shows his sting,
   For talking of their spiritual
Beauty to chorus-girls, for flattering
The features of old gorgons who are rich,
For the impudent grin and Irish charm
   That hides a cold will to do harm,
Today the roles are altered; you must be
The Weaker Sex whose passion is passivity.

The temptation is strong to quote the curiously modern but appropriate speeches of the Wise Men, and the monologue of the bewildered liberal Herod—not to mention the lovely lullaby of Mary—but the examples I have cited are enough to indicate how successfully Mr. Auden has shown the timelessness of the Nativity.

What both of these plays lack is the popular touch. They are the work of high-brows for high-brows. The gap could be at least partly bridged; it is no more impassable than that between the groundlings and the "gods" at the original performances of Shakespeare's plays. In time, if there were sufficient demand, a religious drama could be developed which would appeal to all levels of taste.

The most promising approach might be to start on the folklore or vaudeville level and work up. What I have in mind is a type of play similar to the *Beggar's Opera*. Everything could be thrown into it: prose, verse, dances, ballets, skits. The American musical show, which flourishes with great vitality, could be the jumping-off-place for evolving a religious drama that would be universally meaningful. Such plays could have enough substance to satisfy the highbrows, and enough earthy vigor to interest the low-brows.

Everything that has been said here applies also to the radio. Indeed, in many ways the radio offers still more hopeful possibilities. It is free of many of the technical difficulties that beset the stage manager who is ordered, say, to show a choir of angels hovering in mid-air. The outstanding experiment in radio up to the present is Dorothy Sayers' cycle of plays, *The Man Born to Be King*, written in thoroughly modern prose, and presented a few years ago over the B.B.C. to great popular and critical acclaim.[3]

This whole discussion has been somewhat artificial, for I have confined it to the activities that are conventionally called "arts." The distinction between sculpture and ceramics, and between ceramics and bread-making is not an absolute one. At most, one can say that the traditional "arts" are intense and specialized ways of expressing the creative drive, but that the same drive can be expressed in practically any activity of human life.

There is no person, however ordinary and unimaginative, who cannot co-operate in God's work of creation, once he understands that creativity is part of what it means to be made in the image of God. Raising flowers, making dresses, keeping a scrapbook, photography, wood carving, basket weaving, quilt-making—these are a handful of activities that are creative. But I am speaking as though the work must be a hobby. That is not so. It can be a vocation as well

[3] Published in America in 1949 by Harper & Brothers.

as an avocation. To the creative spirit the task of earning daily bread becomes creative. I grant that it seems far-fetched to apply this to the factory worker who is caught in the treadmill of a mechanical process. This is one of the most cogent arguments against the assembly-line method of production. Society stifles the creative instinct at the risk of seeing it turned into destructive, demonic channels.

One definition—not a complete one—of a Christian society is therefore: a society in which each member knows that he is meant to share in the creativity of God, and has a genuine opportunity to do so.

The Church

Throughout this book I have spoken of "the Church" one moment and "the churches" the next, without any clear distinction. My vacillating usage reflects the guilty conscience characteristic of the Christian world today. The wickedness of a divided Christendom is beginning to be felt, but the divisions remain.

The separate existence of hundreds of competing sects stands condemned for the most practical reasons. It is wasteful; it weakens the impact of Christianity on society; it repels the inquirer who might otherwise be drawn to Christianity. But the greatest condemnation is contained in the prayer of Christ: "Holy Father, keep through,thine own name those whom thou hast given me, that they may be one, as we are."

The situation does not seem as hopeless as a century ago. From the time of the Reformation, the passion for division and subdivision had grown constantly more intense; almost every ambiguous verse in the Bible had been tortured into a justification for a new denomination. Recently, the tide has been gradually turning. The principal Methodist groups in America are now united. The Congregational Church merged with one branch of the Christian Church some years ago, and is now uniting with the Evangelical and

Reformed Church. Other mergers have at least reached the discussion and negotiation stage.

Co-operation short of organic union has progressed with great rapidity. The Federal Council of Churches contains representatives from most of the major Protestant denominations in America, as well as the Episcopal Church and branches of the Orthodox Church. The World Council of Churches, which is a more recent organization, represents about one-fourth of all the Christians in the world, and is open to all churches which profess faith in Christ "as God and Saviour." At its 1948 meeting in Amsterdam every major division of Christendom, with the exception of the Roman Church, was represented.

The final goal, however long it may take, can be nothing less than organic unity. This does not require a highly centralized organization. There can be diversity within the unity—variations in ritual, etc. The parallel between the unity of the Church and the political unity of the world is obvious. But unity, to mean anything, must mean that a Christian minister could serve anywhere in the world without reordination; that individual Christians could go into any church and make their Communions; and that the whole body of believers share the same handful of basic beliefs.

There are two possible approaches to Church unity. One is the "vaguest common denominator." It is doomed from the start, unless one is willing to equate Christianity with humanism. For example, a recent survey conducted among a group of ministers in one particular denomination revealed that they agreed on only one thing: belief in God. Some of them accepted the divinity of Christ, some denied it; some even denied that He had ever lived.

The bare belief in God seems an inadequate basis, unless

the word "Christian" is extended to include the Mohammedans, Jews, and a good many other monotheists. Even this slender basis would have to be abandoned if the Unitarians were to be included. They officially recognize two classes of members: "theists" and "nontheistic humanists."

There *is* a second approach. It begins with a confession: every denomination in existence today is partial, one-sided. Each is trying to make believe that its fragments of the truth are the whole truth. Bonnell Spencer, in his book, *They Saw the Lord,* has stated the situation well:[1]

In this day, when Christendom is so sadly divided, we have much to learn from Paul. Like him before his conversion, we are likely, through devotion to a partial revelation, to reject the fulness of the Gospel. Each of us has been nurtured in one of the many Christian sects. Every Christian group possesses some fragment, large or small, of the totality of Christian truth. No group possesses it all, though for centuries each has been claiming that it does and denying the truth of what some of the others hold. Hence, in the official position of each Christian body, there is to be found some positive truth and some negations of it. If we are content to remain as we are, we adopt the position of Saul the Pharisee. . . .

The road to truth and unity, as Saul discovered, lies in the opposite direction. It is God's will that all the fragments be gathered up and fitted together. Because we have all been raised in a partial Christian tradition, we all have much to learn. We should make a serious effort to comprehend the truths which are enshrined in other traditions and to see how they can be integrated with what we already hold. But it must be a true synthesis in which nothing is discarded on either side except our prejudices and negations.

[1] New York: Morehouse-Gorham Company, 1947, pp. 210-11. Quoted by permission of the publishers.

This is reunion not by subtraction but by addition. Most disagreements over questions of dogma come about, not from what is asserted, but from what is denied. The Unitarian, for example, readily admits that Christ was human; he might learn from his Lutheran friend that Christ is also divine. The Lutheran knows all about the evil of human nature, but the Unitarian could explain to him in what ways human nature is also good. The Quaker is convinced from his own experience that the individual soul can commune directly with God; his Anglican and Roman Catholic friends can explain to him the special purpose of the sacraments as divinely instituted methods of contact.

In none of the instances that I have imagined would any Christian abandon anything but his negations. There are undoubtedly some doctrines, held by certain denominations, which are simply mistaken and cannot be fitted into the totality of truth, but I suspect that they are few and seldom have to do with crucial points. The half-truths, the negations, are the main barriers. A process of addition, continued long enough and with a quite humble desire for the complete truth, would lead to a complete Christianity, with all its fullness and paradoxical tensions.

The process of reunion-by-addition, if I am not mistaken, would lead to a theological basis similar to that usefully, if not completely, expressed in the Apostles' Creed and the Nicene Creed. These ancient formulations do not pretend to contain the whole of Christian truth; they are simply the bedrock foundation, and the individual can well be left free to use his own judgment in the less basic matters of belief. This, again, is diversity within unity.

Whether Christendom will ever be completely united into one Church I shall not try to say. The widest gap of all—that between the Roman Catholic and Protestant faiths

—is very difficult to bridge. At the very least, the strong pull toward unity should eventually result in a considerable reduction in the number of denominations.

Regardless of whether unity comes about, certain problems face every group of believers and similar trends in thought and feeling are evident today in churches that on the surface have very little in common.

One thing is the rediscovery of the idea that Christianity makes sense. This realization had never been lost by the more Catholic-minded churches, but many of the Protestant churches went through a stage of apologizing for theology and dispensing with it as much as possible. Theology is now returning. In the Protestant churches this seems to be taking the form of "neo-orthodoxy," a non-fundamentalist brand of classical Christianity, whose American prophet is Dr. Reinhold Niebuhr. Far from being an enemy of mysticism and personal devotion, theology is the indispensable underpropping; without an intellectually convincing bird's-eye view of religion, its more subjective side is vulnerable to attack from the man who has read the latest book of atheistic philosophy and has a *system* to hurl against an *emotion*. The revival of theology does not mean that the churches are turning their backs on social problems. On the contrary, the social implications of classical Christian theology are considerably more drastic than those of the "social gospel."

A closely associated tendency is a new emphasis on the idea of the Church per se: a rediscovery of what the Church *is*. It is astounding that several generations of Christians, brought up on Paul, should have been able to regard the Church as a sort of Kiwanis Club or women's society. The early theory of the Church, and the only one which has any backing in the New Testament and early Church history, is that of an organism—a more than human "body," uniting the Christians of all times under one head, Christ. With this idea of the Church goes the concept of *sobornost*, as the Russians call it—a word rich in connotations, which can only be clumsily translated as "togetherness." The social implications of the new understanding of the Church are far-reaching: they point toward a society which is neither atomistic individualism nor anthill collectivism. One consequence of the revival of the historic theory of the Church is that Holy Communion, the Church's most characteristic action, has suddenly begun to assume more significance in many denominations. It is both a symbol of *sobornost* and a means of changing the symbol into a reality.

There is a third widespread tendency, which springs, I believe, from at least two causes. One is the realization that Christians will always be divided into two groups (with shadings in between): those who take their religion seriously and those who prefer to drift along with a minimum of personal commitment. The other cause is awareness that it is no longer accurate to speak of "Christian society" in most of America and Europe. As a consequence, the completely committed Christians are faced with responsibility for reaching out and winning over more pagans than lived in the Roman Empire at the time of Paul.

This third tendency, therefore, is toward the formation of small, intensely dedicated groups of people who study their religion together, share their insights and problems, learn from the microcosm what total Christianity might be, and then try to apply it to the macrocosm. These little groups are "cells." Like biological cells, they can grow and subdivide into new cells, until they begin to have a steady impact on the secular world.

The idea is as old as religion. It is based on the psychological fact that the greatest religious progress is made in small groups. One individual by himself is likely to feel bewildered and helpless or else become smug about "the flight of the alone to the Alone." Two hundred people worshiping together in a church can seldom know one another well enough to have an intimate interreaction. In groups ranging, say, from half-a-dozen to twenty-five members, the individuals know one another thoroughly, but the numbers are not so great that a mob psychology, with its crude oversimplifications, arises. Such small "cells" often develop a group mind and group spirit (completely different in quality from the mob mind and mob spirit) and the partial insights of the individual are merged and transmuted into a larger understanding and more vital dedication.

During all the crucial periods when Christianity has shown the greatest life, the cell idea has been strongly in evidence. The twelve apostles were a cell; each early congregation was a cell. The periodic monastic reformations were the work of cells; St. Francis started a cell; the Wesleyan movement began as a cell. The pattern is unmistakable: first the cell, completely dedicated and creating new spiritual vitality, and then the impact on the sluggish Church as a whole and on the pagan world.[2]

There are now more groups of this sort in existence than the average churchman suspects. Certain of them are not specifically Christian. Some of the definitely Christian centers are Pendle Hill, run by the Quakers, in Wallingford, Pennsylvania; Kirkridge, a Presbyterian venture, also in Pennsylvania; and the Congregational-Christian center at Pine Mountain in New Hampshire.

---

[2] Anyone who wishes to know how the cell idea can be adapted to any church tradition should consult Elton Trueblood's admirable book, *Alternative to Futility* (New York: Harper & Brothers, 1948).

Europe, which has felt the impact of anti-Christian ideologies more strongly than America, has a whole network of these centers. Professor Walter M. Horton, of Oberlin College, recently discovered seven of them during one summer in Europe. The oldest—the Sigtuna Foundation in Sweden—dates from 1915. None of the others was founded before the year of Munich.

The most picturesque of the lot is the Iona Movement[3] in Scotland. It is an attempt to take the Incarnation seriously, to use it as the key to reviving Christianity and creating a Christian civilization in Scotland. It was founded in 1938 by Dr. George MacLeod. The center of the Movement is the little island of Iona off the west coast of Scotland. It was here that St. Columba came from Ireland in the sixth century to establish the first Christian mission to the Scots. For three months each summer the members of the brotherhood—ministers and craftsmen—work together at rebuilding the ruined abbey. They share their work, studies, and worship. They learn at first hand the difficulty, rewards, and necessity of making Christianity a total thing.

The island is merely the dramatic focal point and laboratory. The other nine months of the year the members scatter; the ministers to their parishes, the craftsmen to their trades. The group is kept in contact by periodic meetings, by a fixed daily regime of prayer and Bible reading, and by an "economic witness" which requires each member to turn over for group use any income in excess of the

[3] For an account by the founder of the Movement, see George MacLeod, *We Shall Rebuild: The Work of the Iona Community on Mainland and on Island*, The Iona Community, Publishing Department, Community House, 214 Clyde Street, Glasgow C 1. (American edition: Kirkridge, Bangor, Pa.) Shorter descriptions are contained in the *Christian Century* (January 22, 1947 and September 11, 1946), and in *Current Religious Thought* (January, 1946).

national average unless he is prepared to defend in open meeting his use of the surplus for purposes which he considers justified.

The attempt to extend the Incarnation into Scotch life includes down-to-earth activities. In Glasgow, for example, a community center has been erected, with a large library and facilities for meals, meetings, religious services, classes, etc. The Movement has also pioneered in establishing missions in new housing developments and other areas where more timid church leadership holds back.

It goes almost without saying that the Movement has incurred—and with justice—the charge of radicalism. While it does not try to dictate anyone's vote in the elections, it does drive home the importance of intelligent political action, and has much to say about slums, health conditions, and many other matters that some professing Christians would prefer to exclude from the scope of religion. At the same time, the whole tendency is far removed from the vague humanitarianism of the "social gospel." A large part of the experimental work of Dr. MacLeod and his associates has been directed toward restoring the richness of Scotch church life, by reforms in architecture, use of symbolism, a new understanding of Holy Communion, and a modern adaptation of the Church calendar.

The nucleus of the Movement is small. Early in 1947 Dr. MacLeod listed only thirty-four ministers as full members— the number of craftsmen was not given. Around the nucleus were grouped about 180 minister associates and 380 women associates, who observe a "rule" of less intensity.

As our civilization becomes more and more secular, the distinction between Christians and secularists will grow sharper. A process of polarization should ensue. Indeed movements like that of Iona are probably evidence that the process has already begun. One might imagine further steps. A center such as Iona, located on a tract of tillable soil, could develop into a Christian community complete with its own shops and even small factories. Such a community would be a laboratory to test the possibility of creating a Christian society, and would be a place to train Christians who would later go into the secular world as cell organizers.

The obstacles are many and obvious. The members of the community would have to be content with frugal living and simple household equipment. There is also the discouraging record of many experiments in the past—Brook Farm and others. But several things need to be said. These nineteenth-century ventures were planned too much on the drafting board; they did not grow naturally and organically. In the second place, the persons participating were gathered together in hit-or-miss fashion, and had little in common. Finally, the nineteenth century was bathed in so rosy a glow of optimism that the *need* did not seem urgent. Today the need is so great that religious communities would have a better chance of success. And they would not be retreatism. Professor Toynbee has shown the importance of the pattern, "withdrawal-and-return." The Christians who withdrew from secular society to found a Christian community would create a new life which would in time spill over the boundaries into the outside world.

There are also signs that some churches which have been historically hostile to monasticism are rethinking their attitude toward it. A group of French Protestants, to give one instance, has recently established a monastery near Cluny. The Reformation antipathy to monasticism was partly —but only partly—justified. The Reformers were very right to inveigh against the corruption into which so many monasteries and convents had sunk, just as modern political reformers rightly denounce corrupt conditions in city government. But it is one thing to denounce corrupt politics and another to say that there should be no city government at all.

Monasticism is actually a very simple thing. Certain men and women—a rather small number—are by nature suited for a specialized religious life. In order to live it, they are willing to forego much that is normal and good: marriage, for example. There is nothing strange or perverse about this. Scientists and explorers sometimes make the same sacrifices, and are admired for their devotion to a cause greater than themselves.

Medieval monasticism at its best was not a selfish retreat from the "practical world." The monks and nuns were the educators, social workers, and agricultural experts of the time. Despite the growth of the "welfare state," there will always be needs that the state cannot or will not reach. What they will be in the twenty-first century we cannot know. They will probably be very unpleasant or complicated tasks, which the state prefers not to touch. There is no danger that monasticism, adapted to future conditions, would not have urgent work to do.

However, monasticism has another contribution to make. It is one that is peculiarly offensive to current ideas, and the label of selfish retreatism is freely applied. Christianity teaches that prayer is a force. It is not merely that a subjective change occurs in the individual who prays. In some supernatural way his prayer releases a power for good which benefits not only him but others. Some monks and nuns will therefore spend their time in prayer and contemplation and be serving mankind as truly as if they were bandaging wounds.

Gerald Heard, in a passage of remarkable insight, thus comments:[4]

Out on the Mongolian frontiers where three struggling empires wrestle, a traveler lately found a small body of Christian monks serving the desperately harassed native population in their effort to keep body and soul together. The traveler was pleased but not surprised. He was more surprised than pleased to find a little farther on another small group of monks; for these were Contemplatives, given wholly to the task of striving to see God. He asked one of the active monks, "Surely this is hardly the place for Contemplatives?" "On the contrary," replied the active servant of the poor, "we never work save with a group of Contemplatives near us." The active ministrants were the portable batteries to bring faith and life to a tortured, exhausted people. The Contemplatives were the dynamos to recharge the batteries.

My brief sketch of certain modern movements in the Church may have given the impression that the Church of the future will exist mostly for small, intensely devoted groups of believers; that a fully committed Christian should apply for admission at the nearest monastery or convent. Nothing could be more false to the spirit of Christianity or less likely to be the actual situation. Intense Christianity on the part of the small groups is always matched by intensified Christianity among the mass of believers. The small groups are, in Mr. Heard's phrase, the dynamos.

The Church was established by Christ to continue His work after He was no longer visibly present. What He once did in plain daylight, the Church is to do now. The work of Christ was to bring God and man, and man and men, together in complete harmony. To do this was to undo most

[4] *The Code of Christ: An Interpretation of the Beatitudes,* (New York: Harper & Brothers, 1941), p. 147. Quoted by permission of the publishers.

of history, to make a fresh start. The result for the individual is "salvation"; the result for society is that human relations become a closer foreshadowing of what they are meant to be in the Kingdom of God.

It is here that we come to the most important rediscovery of the Church today: its claim to *totality*. By this I do not mean anything remotely resembling totalitarianism. I mean simply a recognition of the fact that Christianity is not a hedged-off flower garden. Christ conceded no obscure corners and crannies of life from which He could be excluded. His teachings, so simple that they could be summarized on a sheet of paper, make unrelenting demands in every human and social situation. The Church, being entrusted with the work and teachings of Christ, can do no less.

The weapons of the Church are the same as those of Christ: truth and love. It is to teach and love mankind into desiring and seeking the complete psychological and social harmony that only obedience to God and love of God can produce. In its teachings the Church must be total. If the living conditions of fruit pickers in California are a denial of the Incarnation, it must say so; if the Negroes of Mississippi or Detroit are treated as second-class citizens, the Church must speak with the prophetic demand for justice. In all things it must hate the sin completely, love the sinner completely, and be ready to bring him to complete forgiveness. And in its effort to make Christianity *total*, it must never forget that external reforms are not enough: the most lasting reform is in each individual, as he catches some glimpse of what Christ is and what Christ offers.

If the Church is uncompromising it will make enemies. Some of them will be outsiders who want the Church to mind its own business. Others will be members who will withdraw their presence and contributions. All this is of no importance. The closer the Church comes to being Christ-in-action, the more it acquires the attributes of Christ. And one of the things about Christ was simply that He could be killed but could not stay dead.

Somehow the Church must learn to convey, as it rarely does today, the utter love, the transforming Grace of God, the passionate glory of Christ's life and death. If it does this, men and women will know the complete joy and abandon that swept the early Christians and has moved the saints through the ages. This cannot be done by beautiful buildings, by large investments, by social respectability, or by deifying the status quo. To the men of His time, Christ was a dangerous revolutionary, not merely in the political but also in the ultimate sense; only the person who has honestly tried to live on even a small scale what Christ taught knows how radical such an attempt is.

There are only two directions in which the Church can go. It can retreat further into its private flower garden, and wait for the world to trample down its protective hedge. Or it can cut down the hedge itself and emerge into the world, to claim all of life for its concern. If it emerges—as it is beginning to show strong signs of doing—it has the promise of its Founder and Head that the gates of hell cannot prevail against it. Its ministers and members may be thought queer; some of them may be martyred; stones may be hurled at stained-glass windows; the Church itself may be suppressed by formal decree. But it will rise again on the third day, stronger and with deepened dedication.

Index

Index

Abolition movement, Christian background of, 101 f.
Abstract art, 36
Adam and Eve, 70, 125
Addams, Jane, 50
After Many a Summer Dies the Swan, 55
Agnosticism, 11, 48, 140
Albertinelli, 45
Alternative to Futility, 173 n.
Anachronism (in art), 161 f.
Analects of Confucius, 143
Anglican Communion, 84, 127, 145, 170; *see also* Church of England *and* Episcopal Church
Anti-Semitism, 107 ff.
Antislavery Impulse: 1830-1844, 102 n.
Apostles' Creed, 170
Aquinas, Thomas, 71, 159
Architecture, 159, 175
Arnold, Matthew, 154
Art for art's sake, 20, 33
Arts, 154 ff.; as barometer of social and cultural changes, 33 ff.
Assembly-line, *see* Mass-production
Atheism, 96, 140, 146, 158, 171
Atomic age, 12 f., 88, 122, 128
Atonement, 56, 71, 116
Auden, W. H., 42, 56, 162 ff.

Bahai, 53 f.
Bahaullah, 53
Baptists, 145
Barnes, Gilbert Hobbs, 102 n.
Beggar's Opera, The, 165
Behaviorism, 29 f.
Bell, B. I., 139 n.
Bentham, Jeremy, 95
Bhagavada-Gita, 143
Bible, 77, 104, 108 f., 142 ff., 171
Bigness, worship of, 84 ff.
"Biological man," 22 ff.
Birth control, 127 f.
Brook Farm, 176
Brotherhood of Man, 47, 101, 108, 111
Brown, Robert M., 14
Buddhism, 56 f., 114, 116

Calvin, Calvinism, 28 f., 65, 145
Capitalism, 81 f., 112, 118
Cartels, 81
Catholicism, 56, 171; *see also* Anglican Communion, Eastern Orthodox Church, *and* Roman Catholic Church
Celibacy, 177
Cells, Christian, 172 ff.
Chaplains, 94 f.
Charity, public, 98 f.
Charles, Clayton H., 14